THE DAY THE SKY FELL DOWN

The Story of the
Stockport Air Disaster

by
Stephen R. Morrin

ISBN 0 9534503 0 9

First published in Great Britain in 1998
by Stephen R. Morrin

Copyright Stephen R. Morrin 1998

Published by Stephen R. Morrin, Stockport.

Printed in Great Britain by
Lithaprint Ltd., Stockport, Cheshire
Telephone 0161 480 1434

This book is

dedicated to the

72 Passengers and Crew

of Argonaut Hotel Golf.

CONTENTS

- *Acknowledgements* -

I would like to thank the following people and organisations for all the wonderful help they have given me over the years, without which this book would not have been possible.

Survivors Vivienne Thornber, David Ralphs and Harold Wood. Rescuers Brian Taylor, John Perkins, Margaret and Patrick Finnigan, Harry Burgess and Brian Quinn. Ex Police Officers Geoff Burgess, Charles Hunt, Roger Gaskell, Bernard Sharrocks and Maurice Sheldrake. Ex Fire Officer Mike Phillips.

Arthur and Bertha Thorniley (Salvation Army), Harry and Bobbie Marlow, Chris McNeill, Jacky Martinez, Ruth Oliver, C. N. Charlesworth, Robert and Chris Hamnett, Barbara Bishop, John Pollard, Helen Cuthew, Melvyn Scorah, Frank Riley, Geoff Rowland, Barrie Dean, Phil Hodgson, Les Jackson and Jill Wood.

David Thorpe for his support over the years and for furnishing me with background information on Julia Partleton. Local aviation historian and writer, Brian Robinson for his encouragement and unlimited access to his records. Steve Cliffe (Stockport Heritage). Barry Bevins, Producer and Director of the BBC documentary 'Aircrash'. Pauline O'Sullivan and Marilyn Bradley for their kind permission to tell their story. David Reid and his staff (Stockport Heritage Library). David Barnaby, my teacher of over thirty years ago for editing the manuscript. Authors, Vic Hallam, Joe Bamford and Arthur Lane for freely giving their advice. Reporters, Bob Greaves and David Hamilton, who recounted their memories for inclusion in the narrative. Grahame N. Elliott CBE and Robert Nadin (British Midland Airways). Air Accidents Investigation Branch, Farnborough. Fredric Robinson Limited, John Prince (Manchester Evening News), Debbie Haile and John Jeffay (Manchester Metro News), Eileen Payne (Stockport Express), Peter Dewhurst (Nelson Leader), Chris Bye (Leeds Evening Post), Mike Wallbank (Express and Chronicle, Huddersfield), Tony Bellshaw (Sheffield Star), Granada Television, BBC Television, Manchester Live TV, GMR Talk Radio, Signal Radio Cheshire, Piccadilly Radio, Radio Five Live.

Special thanks to the Reverend Arthur Connop MBE, not only for writing the foreword to this book, but for his friendship, which I value deeply.

For their help with the memorial, which is also part of this story, I thank Stockport MPs Andrew Stunell and Ann Coffey. Joe Smith and Vanessa Brook of Stockport MBC Community Services for their unstinting efforts. Stonemason Bill Stevenson (Granart Memorials) and Ted McAvoy (Leander Architectural).

I am especially indebted to my friend and fellow campaigner, Brian Donohoe, one of the first rescuers on the scene, who joined with me to fulfil his original vision for a permanent memorial at the site.

Last but not least, my heartfelt thanks to my partner Lynn, for all her patience, encouragement and support she has given me over the years and putting up with my somewhat bizarre behaviour during the research and writing of this book.

- *Foreword* -

Whan an event such as the one detailed in this book occurs, it freezes a moment in time in the minds of those who are caught up in it. For many of those, the memory is indelible. Their lives are changed and they bear the scars in mind or body forever. Beyond them millions of other people are more temporarily affected as news of the tragedy, spreading out like shock waves from an explosion, reaches them through radio, television and newspapers. It awakens horror, distress and sympathy as details of the event unfold but those reactions are not permanent. The story fades in their memories as it is overtaken by the affairs of their own lives, circumstances nearer to them, and sadly by other tragedies and disasters which take over the front page.

Now thirty-one years after the Aircraft plunged from the sky to bring such destruction of life, many living in this Stockport area will have lost clear remembrance of the details of that fateful day. The author of this book is attempting to offer a factual account, which will refresh memories and also inform any who were previously unaware of the tragedy.

In writing this book, Steve Morrin has made it possible for us to have a very accurate record of the circumstances surrounding the tragedy, and an insight into the minds of the survivors and the bereaved, as they have struggled to get on with the rest of their lives. I have some awareness of the tremendous effort which Steve has made to gather together his information. He has made unbelievable efforts to track down the survivors, relatives of the deceased, and anyone who had part in the rescue efforts or who could give any information about the circumstances. He has written innumerable letters, made countless telephone calls and travelled many hundreds of miles to contact his sources. Many of those whom he has contacted, were, like myself, unknown to him but have become his friends. His efforts have resulted in a contribution to the history of our town and a tribute to many of its citizens.

I am certain this book will be a valuable reference for all who read it, and that if any minor inaccuracies do occur they are not due to any lack of endeavour by Steve, so ably and generously supported by his wife Lynn.

Arthur Connop

- Introduction -

1Oam on Sunday 4 June 1967, a British Midland Airways, Canadair C-4 Argonaut airliner - radio call sign Hotel Golf packed with returning holidaymakers from Palma, Majorca, turned onto the approach to Ringway Airport, Manchester. To Captain Harry Marlow and his First Officer Chris Pollard at the controls, it seemed a perfectly normal approach. The slight drizzle and low cloud presented no kind of hazard, yet nine minutes later Hotel Golf lay a tangled, twisted exploding wreck in the centre of Stockport. Of the 84 passengers and crew on board, only 12 survived. What went wrong?

In 1992, just prior to the 25th anniversary of the disaster, I trawled the shelves of Stockport Library searching for information on the accident to augment the little I already knew. Considering this was one of the worst civil aviation accidents at that time and Stockport's greatest catastrophe, I was astonished to find not one single volume which chronicled those events. Even books detailing the history of the town gave it no more than a few lines in passing - a paragraph at most - giving the briefest of details.

On further enquiry at the library counter, I was handed two plain cardboard box files, one contained newspaper cuttings of the time, culled from the local and national press, the other, a collection of black and white photographs which told their own story. Armed with this scant information I began to research this 'forgotten disaster' in depth. At the very beginning I approached the story clinically and without emotion, after all, I was just the researcher and reporter of the events surrounding that fateful first Sunday in June 1967. But, over a period of time as I began to trace and interview all those involved and ultimately meet the relatives of the victims, I became deeply involved in the whole affair which was later to manifest itself in my campaigning for a permanent memorial to those seventy-two passengers and crew who lost their lives.

Researching an event which occurred three decades ago was no easy task. I found it intensely frustrating tracking down individuals, technical records, newsreel footage, photographs and all the relevant documentation needed to give a true and accurate account. That research has uncovered new unpublished facts, which show that the Stockport disaster was an accident waiting to happen. If those facts had been acted upon, the tragic events of Sunday 4 June 1967 could have been averted.

This book is as complete as I can make it, and I hope that it serves two purposes. Firstly as a historical document for the people of Stockport, secondly and more importantly as a lasting memorial to all those who lost their lives in Argonaut Hotel Golf.

Steve Morrin Stockport, 1998

British Midland Argonaut - Hotel Golf

Chapter One

'MY GOD ... HE'S COMING DOWN!'

Sunday morning 4 June 1967, began like any other in Stockport town centre. The rain during the morning, had by ten o'clock given way to light intermittent drizzle, that fell from a sheet of grey overcast which pressed down over the town. Few people were out and about on the wet cobbled streets at that hour, apart from those folk who ventured out for the Sunday papers, and churchgoers on their way to morning worship. In the surrounding streets of terraced houses, housewives cleared away the breakfast dishes and made preparations for Sunday lunch, on what was seemingly going to be just another uneventful day.

At the the newly built police headquarters on Lee Street, officers took refreshments in the canteen, while others on the front desk dealt with the usual mundane police work ... lost dogs and traffic offences.

Outside the Salvation Army Citadel on Middle Hillgate, tambourines jingled, as bandsmen, delayed because of the rain, prepared to set off to play at an old folks home. In just a few minutes time their plans would be forgotten, as they would find themselves engaged in work of a more tragic and dramatic nature.

The events to come were at that very moment being played out above the overcast, drawing ever closer as the minutes ticked by. The people of Stockport were blissfully unaware that death was about to drop out of the sky.

What was about to unfold in the following minutes would wake all these people from their Sunday morning lethargy, and rock Stockport to its very foundations, plunging the town into sorrow, making it the blackest day in its history.

There were numerous eyewitnesses in the outlying areas of Stockport who saw the crippled British Midland Argonaut, struggling to maintain height as it flew on towards the town centre. But only a handful of people were to witness its final death throws and impact into the scrub covered ravine at Hopes Carr.

The Thomas Storey engineering works - world famous for its Bailey Bridges - was situated on higher ground just north east of the town centre at Portwood. Working there that morning on maintenance duties was fitter John Perkins.

'On that particular morning I went to work as normal. It was a 48 hour week in those days and being on maintenance you had to work on Sundays. I was working on the roof of the shot blast unit with Roy Dooley, a chap called Tony and 'Flecker' Clark - we nicknamed him Flecker because everything he said was, "fleckin this ..." and "fleckin that ..."

'It was about 10 o'clock, brew time, and we decided to have our butties. Flecker had been for the brews and brought them up on the roof. We had just started having our breakfast, when we saw the plane coming in low from the Woodbank area, and we all commented on how low it was. It banked over to the right, and we thought, if he didn't straighten up he would hit the gasometer. We then saw it go down out of sight. We screamed - "IT'S GONE DOWN ... IT'S HIT THE BLOODY FLATS!" Flecker yelled, "Come on, let's go."

'We all dived down the ladder. The dust wagon was there in the yard, an old blue Thames Trader, bald tyres, no tax, no insurance. I don't even know if it had brakes! It was one we used around the factory for shifting rubbish. We all jumped on board and roared off through the streets towards the town centre.'

Nearby at the Portwood service station, business was slow due to the wet weather and the early hour. Petrol pump attendant, Harry Delaney, found time to watch the aircraft as they broke through the overcast and traverse the sky over the town centre on their approach and let down into Manchester Airport. But he was totally taken aback when the grey bulk of the Argonaut loomed out of the drizzle at a sickeningly low altitude, on what appeared to him a collision course with the nearby gasometer.

'It banked to the left in a deliberate attempt to miss the gasholder, and then to the right narrowly missing a factory chimney, then it seemed to gain a little altitude before dropping from view behind trees beyond St Mary's Church.'

Alarmed that the aircraft might have hit the Covent Garden flats where his wife was at home, Harry Delaney immediately left work and rushed home.

Meanwhile, nearer the town centre, Patrick Finnigan leaned into the drizzle as he walked to work down Upper Brook Street with his 10 year old son Martin. Mr Finnigan, a boiler man for Nixons on Hopes Carr, made this journey every Sunday morning with his two sons, who would help collect coal in the wheelbarrow for him as he tended to the boiler. But because of the rain that morning he decided to leave his youngest son at home.

Reaching the end of the street, they crossed over Waterloo Road, taking a short cut between the old houses and the patch of waste ground which lay behind the Hopes Carr sub-station. Arriving at the front door of the premises, Patrick Finnigan fumbled with the keys as he prepared to open up. For his son Martin, standing on the pavement outside, the next few minutes would be the most dramatic in his young life.

One police officer not taking refreshments in the canteen that morning, was motorcycle patrolman Bill Oliver. At 10:08, he turned his machine into Waterloo Road from the Hillgate end and slowly rode down the dip towards its junction with Hopes Carr. As he drew alongside the Waterloo Hotel, he saw the unbelievable sight of a large four engine airliner flying diagonally towards him. At no more than sixty feet, the Argonaut scraped over the roof of the Herbert Parks Tool Works. Bill Oliver brought his motorcycle to an abrupt halt and sat transfixed as the sudden realisation hit him ... 'MY GOD ... HE'S COMING DOWN!'

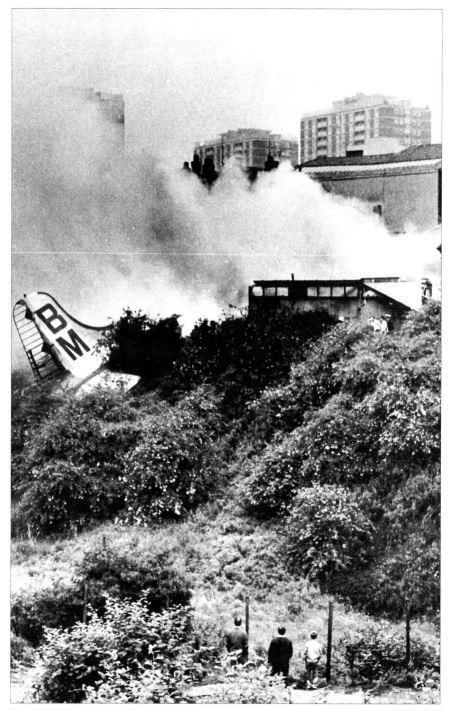

Hotel Golf ablaze minutes after impact   (Stockport Express)

Chapter Two

THE DAY THE SKY FELL DOWN

PC Bill Oliver stared in stunned disbelief as Hotel Golf swept diagonally towards him over Waterloo Road. Thinking the aircraft would hit the buildings he was coming up against, he turned right into the mouth of Canal Street in an effort to avoid the inevitable crash. As he did so he heard the dreadful sound of impact - the tearing scream of metal as the port wing scythed into the gable end of a two storey terrace, ripping it away complete with engines, demolishing part of the building and setting it on fire.

The rest of the aircraft pancaked onto a long, low concrete garage containing a dozen cars and vans, overturning some of them, and causing several incipient petrol fires. The passenger cabin floor shattered on impact, ripping seats from their mountings and hurling some passengers through the gaping hole where the port wing had been torn away. Hotel Golf finally came to a stop when the right wing buried itself into the back wall of the Hopes Carr sub-station cutting electrical power to the surrounding area. The cockpit, almost severed from the main fuselage, lay crumpled and battered against the sub-station side wall, spilling its guts of instrumentation and wiring over the garage forecourt. The tail section was left projecting over the edge of the steep scrub-covered slope of the ravine that led down to the stream below.

The pandemonium of noise suddenly ceased, there was now complete silence. Small fires had broken out here and there, and a pall of black smoke spiralled upwards from the shattered airliner. Everywhere around the crash scene the pungent smell of aviation fuel hung heavily in the air.

Patrick Finnigan had just opened the door of Nixons and was about to enter, when without any warning Hotel Golf struck the ground only yards away, the noise was horrendous. Martin screamed, "DAD, A PLANE JUST FELL OUT OF THE SKY!"

Without hesitation Patrick Finnigan ran with his son the short distance to the scene to lend what assistance he could.

Noise of the impact was heard by Alan Key, landlord of the Waterloo Hotel, diagonally opposite the scene of the crash.

'We heard the whole explosion. At first it sounded like thunder, then the building shook and I thought it was more like a lorry crash. I looked out of the window and saw a mass of smoke and flames and a man on his hands and knees crawling away. I then thought it was a workshop explosion. Police and civilian workmen arrived on the scene within seconds.'

Teenage brothers, Robert and Chris Hamnett, were walking down Spring Gardens on their way to St Mary's church. As they approached its junction with Waterloo Road a whistling noise made them turn and look over their shoulders:

'It flew right over us - it was massive. As it passed over the pub on the corner the turbulence dislodged a chimney pot. We just threw ourselves to the ground.'

On hearing the sound of impact down in Hopes Carr, Robert and Chris picked themselves up and ran across Spring Gardens into Waterloo Road.

'We ran all the way down on the right hand side, to where the gate is at the end of the iron railings. Three men ran across the road, brushed past us and tried to open the gate, but the gate was locked. The men didn't hesitate, they clambered over and made their way down to the stream at the bottom.

'Then we saw the stewardess, she was out amazingly quickly, she jumped down into the bushes, stumbling and falling all the way down the opposite slope. She didn't want any help at all when the men reached her, she told them, "Leave me alone, I'm alright, you see to the others."

'We were too young to react and absolutely stunned and shocked by it all. We couldn't believe what was there in front of us. We only stayed a few minutes before going on to church. When we told people what had happened they didn't believe us. No one believed us.'

Stewardess Julia Partleton's last recollection before the crash was standing in the galley, getting a glass of water for a passenger who was feeling unwell.

'I don't remember turning the taps off.' She said, 'The next thing I remember is lying on the ground some way from the plane, with my clothes alight. I could see the tail of the aircraft sitting up in the air. As I lay there I heard screaming and a loud explosion coming from the plane.'

PC Bill Oliver, shocked by the violence of what he had just witnessed, immediately radioed police headquarters which was only a few hundred yards away. As soon as his call was acknowledged he ran into Hopes Carr with three or four other men who saw the crash and dashed to the scene.

Approaching the wreckage through the swirling smoke he was totally unprepared for the scene of appalling devastation which lay before him.

'As I got close to it, I saw a man dressed in a blue suit staggering away. He appeared to be dazed. He was about five yards from the crashed plane, close to the petrol pumps. He looked about fifty odd years of age and had a cut on one side of his head. I told him to get away from the plane as I carried on towards it.

'I could see exposed to my view between twenty and thirty people, due to the large hole in the fuselage caused by the port wing being torn away. At this time it was dead quiet and all the passengers appeared to be seated, facing towards the front of the aircraft. The seats had concertinaed from the rear of the plane. There didn't appear to be any gangway between the seats but they were roughly in rows all across the floor of the plane.

'I saw that some of the passengers were obviously alive and I saw a girl had started to move. I went into the wreckage to get her out.'

That girl was 20 year old Vivienne Werrett from Nelson, Lancashire. Bill Oliver told her later.

'You made such a hell of a noise screaming and shouting, that's why I went to you first.'

Vivienne and her friend, Susan Howarth were sitting on the second row from the front on the starboard side. Vivienne, who was knocked unconscious when the aircraft crashed, says, 'It must only have been seconds, because I regained consciousness very, very quickly, and I saw what I thought was the cabin door swinging, and just in front of that door - flames coming towards me. I don't know where they were coming from. I just looked - it was like you were dreaming. I thought, if I don't do something I'm going to be burnt alive here. I screamed, or tried to. I thought there's nothing coming out - like you do in dreams when you are trying so hard to make a noise and nothing comes.

'That was the last thing I remember until I heard somebody shout, "Oh my God Bill, watch her legs!" Then someone was on my right side, with their hands under my arms trying to pull me out and I was screaming that my legs were trapped.'

Vivienne passed out again as Bill Oliver, now joined by PC John Heath pulled her clear of the tangled wreckage. Carried to the garage forecourt area she was put into the back of a police car and taken the half mile to Stockport Infirmary.

They then freed her holiday companion, Susan.

'I don't remember anything,' she said, 'until we were dragged out of the plane, hearing people screaming and people rushing towards the plane smelling the smoke and hearing the fire crackle, really that's about all.'

Baker, Brian Donohoe, was reading the Sunday papers in the back kitchen above his shop in Middle Hillgate, when he heard the sound of the impact. His first thoughts were that the garage or sub-station had gone up. Thirty years on he recalls the events.

'It was just past ten o'clock, when I heard a dull thud. I looked through the kitchen window - there was some smoke down in Hopes Carr, but not a tremendous amount - I was dressed, but still had slippers on, so I ran downstairs out into the yard. When I got to the bottom of the yard one or two bobbies who I knew were running down the street. I asked, What's up lads? They said, "There's been a plane crash Brian."

'I ran down the street with them, and as I got near the bottom of Watson Square, there was this chap wandering up in a blue suit with a box camera around his neck. One of the bobbies shouted, "Grab hold of him Brian." He had a little trickle of blood from his forehead. We eventually found out his name was Albert Owen from the Wirral and it seems his wife died in the crash. He had actually walked out of the gap in the plane. So I got hold of him and took him back down to the garage forecourt and tied him with the box camera to a petrol pump - which I suppose was not the best idea at the time - but that's where I tied him.

'The cockpit was resting on the edge of the sub-station and one thing I always remember about it was the amount of electric wiring hanging around. Then I saw this gap in the aircraft and waded in.

The battered cockpit rests against the sub-station wall (Stockport Express)

'The first one I got out was 15 year old Fiona Child - I believe she was the farthest back of the survivors. By this time, one or two police cars had arrived, and I carried her to one which took her to the infirmary. The police wanted me to go with her, but I said no, no, I can go back in.'

Fiona said of the crash, 'I woke up just before we crashed and looked out of the window. It felt as if we were drifting. The roofs of the houses were very near. There was no warning. Suddenly the plane started to judder, I don't know what happened, I just remember being upside down suspended by my seat belt and seeing flames.' Fiona regained consciousness as she entered the infirmary, just long enough to whisper her name to a porter, and tell him her mother was waiting for her at the airport.

Clambering over a mass of twisted wreckage and flattened cars, Brian re-entered the fuselage and managed to release 50 year old Linda Parry from Preston. She said, 'I woke up halfway down my seat, and Mary (Green) on the floor beside me. I just saw the wing and the seats in front of us and... open air! I passed out again and I don't remember anything after that until I was in the infirmary.'

Her friend, Mary Green said, 'Everything went round, there seemed to be

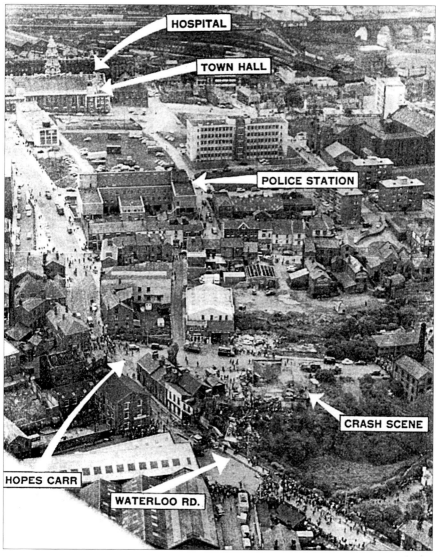

a lot of noise and banging. I blacked out, and the next thing Mrs Parry - who was sitting next to me - said, "Will you unfasten your seat belt." When I looked down I was on fire all down one side. I thought, I'm going to get roasted here because I couldn't use either arm. There was a man hanging over me, who I found out later was a policeman, he must have got me undone. He carried me away from the aeroplane and was stepping over bodies as he went. I was put into a police car and went to the infirmary from there.'

Fourteen year old Harold Wood occupied the window seat overlooking the starboard wing, next to him was his younger brother Bill. Their father, who accompanied them had taken a vacant seat at the front of the aircraft. Harold recalls the moments just after the crash. 'I woke up in the aircraft realising that we had actually crashed and there were flames all around me. My immediate thought was to get out of the aircraft, so I unbuckled my seat belt, walked around the back of my seat to try and get my brother out. I leaned over Bill to undo his seat belt, but he could not move because his legs were pinned by the seats in front, which had come back on him. I can remember walking through the hole in the side of the plane and into daylight. I saw a police car and a policeman walking towards me, he said, "Are you all right?" I shouted, MY BROTHER'S IN THERE, GET HIM OUT.

'At this point I must have collapsed, because my next recollection was being put into the front of a police car. I can remember Fiona Child was in the back of the car. The next time I saw Bill, he was on a trolley in casualty. He had cuts to his head and legs and was bleeding a lot. It was over a week before we were told that Dad had been killed, but to be honest I think we already knew.'

Meanwhile, a few hundred yards away, outside the Hillgate Citadel, the Salvation Army Band prepared to set off. Arthur Thorniley, corps secretary, takes up the story.

'On that first Sunday in June, thirty years ago, the band was just about to leave to go to an open air stand, which we did every Sunday. But because of the rain, it wasn't heavy rain, but it was drizzling - because of that we decided to go and play at one of the old folks homes in the area.

'Just as we were about to leave, a

Salvation Army Band outside Hillgate Citadel (Arthur Thorniley)

white faced youngster came chasing round the Hillgate and stopped at the Mottram Street corner, at the front door of our building and said, "THERE'S A PLANE CRASHED ... DOWN IN WATERLOO!" Those were his words, and we could hardly believe it, because we hadn't heard any crash or anything of that nature. There was no volume of sound in any respect, probably because of the weather.

'However, a number of us dashed round, and there was the plane, lying, wing tipped up and the main fuselage settled down on what I thought were petrol pumps. The only policeman I saw was Bill Oliver, he was on the scene immediately, and as far as I could see he had radioed the police station, which was only a hundred yards away.

'Within what I would think was about a quarter of an hour, all sorts of services were there; the fire brigade, the ambulances and the police in force. Ten or twelve of our bandsmen were there, helping to do what they could to take out the people who were in the plane.'

By this time more police and local residents had arrived at the scene of carnage, and together with Salvation Army bandsmen they clawed at the wreckage like ants in a desperate effort to release the survivors.

In the Stockport ambulance station control room, Mr Goodwin, shift leader that morning, received a telephone call from the police at 10:22, informing him that a four engine aircraft had crashed in the vicinity of Waterloo Road and Upper Brook Street. He immediately called the Ambulance Superintendent and brought into operation the procedure for dealing with a major disaster.

In the ambulance station ten men were on duty manning five vehicles, which was the normal Sunday compliment. Cheshire County and Manchester services were notified and requested to send all available ambulances to the scene. Stockport Infirmary and Stepping Hill Hospital were alerted, extra staff were sent for and all routine work was suspended temporarily. Three vehicles which were already out were redirected, and within minutes four ambulances were at the scene and assisting in the rescue operation.

By 10:45 twenty-two ambulances were in operation - nine from

Manchester, six from Cheshire County and seven from Stockport. Thirteen off-duty ambulance men and two shift leaders reported for duty, this made it possible to send seven vehicles to the crash and also maintain normal routine working. Apart from Cheshire County and Manchester, offers of help were also received from New Mills, Rochdale, Blackburn and Oldham.

A considerable number of police, fire and ambulance personnel, who were off duty, either went straight to the scene or reported to their headquarters, where their offers of help were accepted. Some police officers who were alerted by telephone, at first thought that their Sunday was being disturbed by a civil defence exercise, only to find that what was normally a routine drill, had become tragic fact.

John Perkins and his workmates who saw the aircraft come down and rushed off in the dust wagon from the Thomas Storey factory were now nearing the disaster scene.

'We came down Wellington Street, and were just about to turn to go up

Rescuers claw desperately at the shattered cockpit   (Stockport Express)

13

Hillgate when we saw the smoke and turned into Hopes Carr. We drove up, stopped the wagon and jumped down.

'There was no fire when we arrived, just a bit of smoke. There was an ambulance in the middle of the road and I saw a bobby and a couple of other people there, and people running down from the police station. As we went over there were flattened cars all piled up in the garage. Roy Dooley, who was an auxiliary fireman said: "Be careful here lads, we've got petrol pumps, electrics from the damaged sub-station, a crashed plane and a load of cars all flat - there's going to be fuel hanging about."

'The tail-plane section seemed to be missing, as were parts of the wings. As we climbed up into the fuselage, I saw an ambulanceman helping the stewardess up the grass banking from the stream below. She was screaming and crying. The clothing on her back had been on fire and was still smouldering. He put a blanket around her shoulders and I think she was then taken to the infirmary. Inside the fuselage all the seats were ripped from the floor and piled up down one end against the cockpit door. Most of the passengers seemed to be alive and we began to pull them out - we brought one out still strapped to his seat! All the time there were moans of, "help me" and screams. By this time there were three or four pairs of people going in to help - you couldn't get many in because it wasn't that big a plane inside.

'I think in my naivety, being so young, none of this I was seeing clicked with me, but what did click was the two young teenage brothers (Harold and Billy Wood). They were shocked and stunned, staring ahead as if paralysed.

'We then tried to see if we could get into the cockpit from inside, Roy Dooley went to the front of the plane clambering over cars as he went. He found a hole underneath and with Flecker, they began pulling at it with their bare hands. Roy then went away and came back with a length of scaffolding pole and began bashing at it. We were just about to go back into the fuselage when there was an almighty fireball, you could hear it - like a whooshing noise - the aircraft burst into flames and we were forced back. By this time the fire brigade had arrived and started to cover it in foam.'

Meanwhile PC Bill Oliver continued to pass out the dead and injured:

'The operation of removing people was made more difficult by their legs being trapped under their own seats. Some had broken away from their mountings, and others were twisted on their frames. I remember carrying a small boy, who I think was dead. Throughout this time I did not consciously remember going away from the plane, but passed survivors to some other person who took them away behind me. About this time other police arrived. Among those I remember seeing were the Chief Constable, Deputy Chief Constable and Inspector Marsland.

'There were then two separate explosions close together on the other side of the plane from where I was, and a flash of flame. After the initial flash the flames seemed to lessen, and further rescues were attempted.

'The last person I remember leaving this portion of the plane was a male about forty five years of age, with dark hair. He came up from inside the front of the broken part, some-where between the back of the cockpit and the break in the fuselage, the clothing on his back was on fire.

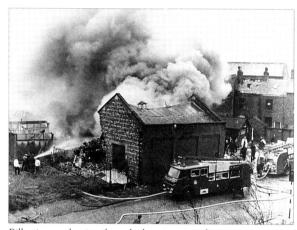

'The fire then seemed to be coming from under where the passengers were, and it

Billowing smoke rises from the burning aircraft as firemen desperately fight the blaze (Stockport Express)

soon became unbearable, but the cockpit did not appear to catch fire at this stage, and the pilot and co-pilot were brought out, but I do not think I assisted in this.

'The heat intensified, and seemed to be burning directly under the passengers more and more, and we were forced to go back. From inside the plane I heard someone scream, "I'm burning!" On retreating from the near vicinity of the plane, I looked into Hopes Carr and saw that fire appliances and ambulances were present, but I am not able to say at what specific stage in the operation they first arrived.

'The plane was now burning fiercely and completely out of control.'

At one point Bill Oliver was working so close to the fire his uniform began to smoulder and burn, firemen quickly hosed him down.

Another rescuer early on the scene was Brian Taylor. He and his brother had just turned into Waterloo Road travelling towards Hillgate, only minutes after the crash.

'As we drove down Waterloo Road we saw the wreckage on the far embankment. There was a lot of smoke about. My brother, who was a bit panic stricken said, "What should we do?" I said, Hang on, I'm going over. I climbed over the railings and jumped down, then made my way up the slope and tried to get between the breakage in the plane. There was at this point no real fire.

'There must have been a couple of dozen people as I can remember, each one doing what they could for the passengers. Then came the fire - it was not so much an explosion but more a whoosh, like throwing petrol on a fire. I could see the passengers at the windows, their hair burning away in an instant. We got a couple of people out and took them to the footpath, I don't know if they were alive or dead. Then the fire brigade, police and everybody else began to arrive and brought in stretchers - before that we had just used old bits of board and corrugated iron. During the fire I tried to pick a spot where it didn't look as hot, but it was impossible, there were thick clouds of black smoke. I remember it burning my nostrils. I had my best check jacket on with it being a Sunday - I remember putting it around a young woman whose hair was burnt, I got her out, and then somebody took over.

'It was one of those situations where there seemed to be so many people being so helpful, it was marvellous, even though it was so horrific. There was a great deal of bravery down there, not just on my part, but by all the people who assisted in the rescue that day.'

After pulling clear Fiona Child and Linda Parry, Brian Donohoe attempted further rescues.

'I went in again and tried to release a lady, she was still strapped in, her ankles were embedded in the footrest. I managed to release them, but I couldn't quite get her out. Eventually I did manage to get her to where the hole in the plane was. Charlie Holt, one of the bobbies got hold of me by the shirt tails and said, "There's explosions Brian." I looked up and there were little explosions coming along the plane, bang, bang, bang, bang, bits of flame, bits of fires happening. By this time I had managed to put the woman onto an empty seat near one of the windows. Charlie Holt who saw that the aircraft was about to explode pulled me so hard by my shirt tails that I released my grip on her. We both went flying to the ground. Where we had been exploded and burst into flames, there was a lot of smoke. When we looked through the cabin window the woman was starting to come round.'

They both watched helplessly as she disappeared from view as the fuselage was enveloped in flames.

For Arthur O'Neill what should have been a happy Sunday, suddenly dissolved when news of the disaster came. Arthur, a Salvation Army Major, described the scene that greeted him.

'It was an absolute hell and an inferno, just a wall of flames. I could see all the people clearly. They seemed to be sitting there looking at us. Suddenly we were aware of our own bandsmen moving in with others, trying to rescue people. They were tremendous as they went into the plane together, because all the time there were explosions.

'There was one man in great distress, he said to me, "My feet are burning - please take my shoes off." I held his hand. He asked me about someone else, obviously a relative. Then there was a young teenage lad in a state of deep shock, he couldn't speak, except with his eyes, so I held his hand too. I sat there holding both their hands.

'It was sheer horror, because the whole fuselage from behind the cockpit had split open. There were people just sitting there enveloped in flames, their clothes were on fire. Some were half naked because their clothes had burned off them. Then there was a lovely little girl of seven or eight brought out, she was really pretty and I thought I detected a movement - I think - I hope, she was alive. She brought home to all of us the fact that this was a family plane.

'The injured were lying all around unable to talk. They just lay there watching the flames lick at the aircraft. I can't help thinking of the rescuers. There were people in blue overalls, obviously from the garage nearby, young policemen, our bandsmen and local folk. Suddenly, they had forgotten everything to face that inferno.'

The Argonaut, on impact broke into three parts. The cockpit crashed onto the garage forecourt up against the sub-station and within ten feet of two 500 gallon underground petrol storage tanks, each almost full and two

Rescuers sift the wreckage as firemen fight the blaze   (Stockport Express)

electric delivery pumps. The starboard wing was embedded in the back wall of the sub-station, which contained two transformers with an input of 6,600 volts. These in turn caught fire and the electricity supply failed over a large area of central Stockport.

The initial call to the Fire Brigade Control was received at 10:12 by an emergency 2222 telephone call from the police. Two appliances were immediately dispatched from Whitehill Street Station under the command of Station Officer Fred Matkin, and a water tender from King Street West which was first to arrive at 10:17. They found rescue operations in progress and the main fuselage and surrounding buildings burning fiercely. Immediately two jets were positioned to cover and protect the rescue workers who, although working in a restricted area, were making good progress. The appliances from Whitehill Street arrived at 10:25 and Chief Fire Officer, Fred Matkin took command, ordering two more jets on the burning wreckage. A water tender from Cheshire Fire Brigade arrived and a further two jets were put to work bringing the total to six. Appliances were now arriving from Manchester Fire Brigade and Manchester airport reported two foam tenders on the way.

During this time the buildings damaged by the aircraft as it crashed were ablaze, and the necessary steps were taken to bring these fires under control. One jet was positioned outside the electricity sub-station until the incoming power was cut off, and two jets were directed on the burning buildings which consisted of offices and a warehouse. Foam jets and additional water were kept in reserve, in anticipation of a serious fire developing in the underground petrol storage tanks, in the garage forecourt area. In the event only one foam tender was actually used, although at one period three were standing by. As a result of these efforts the storage tanks were not involved.

On the arrival of supporting appliances it was realised that the water supply from the mains was limited. This was due to a weekend pressure reduction. Control contacted the water board to obtain an increased supply. However, it became necessary to run a relay from Wellington Road South, a quarter of a mile away.

A number of firemen assisted the police and members of the public in rescue operations. During this work several explosions took place caused by the fuel tanks of vehicles in the wrecked garage. This danger was totally ignored by all concerned.

Chief Fire Officer, Fred Matkin said, 'All those working at close quarters had to bear up in the face of terrible sights of death and injury as they tried to get into the blazing fuselage.'

Some twenty minutes after the crash, attempts were made to extricate the crew. This proved difficult as most of this area was instrument lined and extremely difficult to penetrate. The cockpit section, although not seriously affected by fire was now beginning to burn. Ultimately, hatchets were used to force a hole in the top and side of the cockpit, through which the pilots were rescued.

One Fire Officer who turned out that morning was 21 year old Mike Phillips.

'At the time of the disaster I had been in the Fire Service for two years, joining the Lancashire County Brigade in July 1965 aged 19. I then transferred to the Stockport Brigade at Mersey Square in February 1967 before moving on to Whitehill Street the following April.

'I had never seen a dead body before the air crash, and with 72 people losing their lives in one incident, it was absolutely horrendous. All the training in the world does not prepare you for anything like the job that faced us on the 4 June 1967.

'I was orderly that day and there were quite a few people to cook for. I remember the meat was actually burning and smoke pouring out of the oven - I was no cook! - when the klaxon which turned us out went off. The voice of the firewoman in the control room came over the tannoy: "Plane crash ... Hopes Carr." We all looked at each other and jumped up on the appliances. We set off thinking that it was a false alarm, but when we got to the top of Lancashire Hill we could see a pall of black smoke. We thought it might be a light aircraft. My mind was now working overtime as to what we were going to be faced with, but I was with a great bunch of lads who were older and more experienced than me, and you have to have confidence in the officers and men you are working with.

'By the time we turned into Hopes Carr, the King Street water tender was already there facing us. The scene was unbelievable. I remember people in suits as if they were on their way to church pointing frantically at the blazing aircraft and screaming at us - "THERE ARE PEOPLE IN THERE!" It was dreadful. There were bodies strewn all over the place. I remember seeing a small boy lying there without a mark on him, he was dead!

'I was told to get a jet to work on the burning fuselage. When the hose had been run out and a branch inserted we got water on and Sub-Officer Gregory and myself proceeded forward. We were stumbling over bodies trying to get to the burning wreckage - it was unreal.

'It seemed when we first arrived and got to work there were only a few people watching us. Perhaps we were too engrossed and working on adrenalin to notice, but I remember at one point looking up - it was like an amphitheatre - there were hundreds of people all around, TV cameras, reporters and ice-cream vans.

'Later in the day I had to get some salvage sheets off the appliance and cover bodies. To see them all lined up on the ground was horrendous. I looked at Mick Hurst, a fireman from King Street who was considered a 'hard nut' - he was as pale as I was. At the time I was a young 21 year old. I had been in the Royal Marine Band from the age of 15, I then took a couple of factory jobs until I joined the Fire Brigade. I was naive, innocent and suddenly all this was happening.

'It must have been 16:00 hours before we returned to Whitehill Street. I remember scrubbing down with the lads in the washroom, mostly in silence. I went off duty at 18:00 hours and had arranged that evening to go ten pin bowling at Belle Vue with my mate Derek and our girlfriends. We did go, but it was a dour event because of my state of mind - I was not very good company.

F.O. Mike Phillips   (Mike Phillips)

'For the next 12 months I had nightmares and flashbacks. There was no counselling in those days. It has left an imprint on my mind and I was only a rescuer who arrived after the fire started. The people who saw the faces of those poor passengers must have suffered far more than I did. I have blotted out most of the work I did that day, and I have worked hard since to forget.'

Weeks later, after all the wreckage had been cleared, Mike Phillips found himself back at Hopes Carr on hydrant duty. Scrabbling around in the grass he found peseta coins trodden in the ground - a grim reminder of where the aircraft came from.

There were dramatic scenes at Stockport Infirmary on hearing news of the crash. The hospital's major accident unit went into operation. The unit was headed by the senior orthopaedic surgeon, and by an amazing coincidence he was on his way to the hospital and passing the crash scene, so was able to make an immediate assessment of the situation.

The whole of Holden Ward was cleared and for the first time in its history, men, women and children shared the same ward. It was group therapy at its most basic, each taking comfort in each other and the nursing staff, which greatly eased the ordeal that they had been through.

By 10:45, additional staff began to arrive, and staff from other hospitals came and volunteered their services, as well as other people who came to donate blood. Both operating theatres were put into full use, nine of the survivors had emergency operations, and Julia Partleton the stewardess, who suffered extensive burns, underwent a major operation.

Soon after the ruptured fuel tanks exploded, the fire developed rapidly and within a few minutes engulfed the entire plane. Flames and choking black smoke, fuelled by the cabin furnishings, billowed from the fuselage. The fire was so intense the cabin structure literally melted, the tail section broke away and subsided down the slope.

A solitary policeman surveys the grim scene   (Stockport Express)

22

PC William Davies said, 'What I will never forget were the shouts for help, and the agony on the faces of passengers who screamed from behind the cabin windows. We could not get near because of the intense heat both from the aircraft and the buildings on Waterloo Road.'

Another rescuer said, 'I looked at the tail section and saw about twenty people at the windows. I could hear faint screams for help. Before I could do anything a sheet of flames ripped along the fuselage - they just disappeared from view.'

The rescuers beaten back by the intense heat, could only watch helplessly as trapped passengers beat at the cabin windows pleading for help. The irony was, that after surviving the initial impact, they were to perish in the ensuing fire.

There were now no more screams for help, just the crackle of flames as the entire aircraft was consumed. With all hope gone, the rescuers came away exhausted with the hopelessness of it all. Some sat down at the roadside and wept.

Ambulances line up to rush the injured to hospital as hundreds of onlookers survey the scene of devastation.

(Stockport Express)

24

Chapter Three

AFTERMATH

When the fire was brought under control the rescuers went back into the smoking wreckage with the blind hope of finding some still alive. All they could do now was disgorge the Argonaut's ghastly cargo. There were poignant scenes, as stretcher after stretcher was carried away bearing the blanket shrouded figures of the dead. The passenger cabin was unrecognisable, just mangled blackened aluminium sheeting and the twisted metal framing of the seats. When rescue work was concentrated on the rear of the aircraft, a pile of bodies was uncovered, all subjected to extreme burning. Remarkably, certain items survived - a bottle of sun tan lotion, a straw hat worn in the sun, a packet of duty free cigarettes, a child's doll, a group of handbags and shoes. They were all carefully gathered together on canvas salvage sheets and taken away.

Poignant scenes as stretcher after stretcher is carried away from the wreckage (Stockport Express)

Of the 84 passengers and crew on board, only 12 survived, including the pilot, Captain Harry Marlow. They had all been taken to Stockport Infirmary where a team of 12 doctors and countless nurses worked tirelessly throughout the day. Although they all suffered varying degrees of injury, none were in danger of losing their lives.

PC Roger Gaskell was the Coroner's Officer with Stockport Police. In the coming week he would become deeply involved in the aftermath of the disaster, dealing with the subsequent post-mortems and identification of the 72 victims.

'On that particular morning I was at my mother's house when I received a telephone call from my wife telling me that Sergeant Jones had just knocked on the door and informed her that an aircraft had crashed in Stockport. With that I put on my coat and set off. As I reached the top of the drive one of our lads, Walter Caldwell, was passing in a CID car. He stopped and asked where I was going. I told him an aircraft had crashed in Hopes Carr, he said, "Your joking, we're doing a watching job there at a carpet warehouse, we've had some information that there's going to be a break in."

'We drove to the scene down Hall Street and turned left into Upper Brook Street. As we got to the end of the road it was packed with people. Walter said, "Jump out while I find somewhere to park." I went to the edge of the crowd and saw a sergeant and two PCs on crowd control. Bill Gathercole, who was the sergeant said, "Get over to Yates's garage straight away." I arrived at the garage just as they were bringing in the first bodies. Sergeant Jones was there. He gave me a pile of plastic bags and told me to check the bodies for property, put it in the bags and tie them to the wrists. We had nothing else at that moment. As the bodies started to come in a nursing sister appeared. Where she came from I have no idea. She asked me if there was anything she could do. I told her exactly what Sergeant Jones had told me. We were then joined by two lads from the Regional Crime Squad, Sergeant Dick Evans and a PC from Stockport called Fred Sharpe, who again asked if they could help. I passed on the same instructions.

'After a short time it became apparent that we were not going to have enough room for all the bodies. Sergeant Jones said they were thinking of taking some up to the Salvation Army Citadel on Hillgate. We brought a few more in then went around looking for anything in the way of property and belongings.

Stretchers wait to fulfil their grim task (Stockport Express)

We tidied up, put a uniformed bobby on the front of the garage and went up to the Citadel. When we arrived the whole area had been cleared and bodies laid out covered with white plastic sheeting. By this time all the casualties had been taken out of the plane and everyone was now at the Citadel. The Chief Constable and a lot of the town's dignitaries put their heads together and realised that this was not a satisfactory situation. I don't know who made the decision but it was decided to move all the bodies to the Centenary Hall which was the old Sunday School and not far from the police station.

'Later in the afternoon, two RAF pathologists arrived, Group Captain Mason and Squadron Leader Tarlton. They just turned up at the police station and introduced themselves. It was amazing, the speed of events that Sunday. I took them down to the scene of the crash. By this time Hillgate was like Blackpool Prom, parents with kids on their shoulders, ice-cream vans, burger vans. It was unbelievable. We then went back to the Chief's office, where some representatives from British Midland had now arrived and the Chief went absolutely ballistic because they hadn't got a passenger list. Apparently they were waiting for one to be sent over from Palma. Then we all sat down and decided what the plan of campaign would be on the Monday.'

Immediately after the crash, one section of the town worked with devotion. They were members of the Salvation Army Hillgate Citadel, who maintained contact with the rescuers, ran messages and supplied endless cups of tea and personal comfort to all those involved. Arthur Thorniley, Salvation Army bandsman, recalls his involvement immediately after the fire.

Arthur Thorniley

'I spoke to a policeman, who informed me that as far as he knew there was no mortuary available to accommodate all the 72 victims. So I said to him, I will go and open the Sunday School at the Salvation Army Citadel and clear out the forms with a view to using that as a basis. By this time bodies were being taken across the road to Yates's garage, which was almost opposite the crash site. Probably an hour afterwards - which at that time would be getting on for 11:30 - the police started to arrive at the Citadel. The crowds were so vast that we had to put forms outside to keep the area clear for the ambulances bringing the casualties to the hall. I must say at this time I was away from the crash site dealing with documentation, I was there to place, as circumstances made it available, identification adjacent the bodies.

'The day went on and before we knew, it was early afternoon. Crowds were becoming immense outside the Citadel. It was as if we were giving something away. There were thousands, thousands of people and before long vendors arrived selling burgers, ice-cream, you name it - it was like the entrance to a football ground - it rather took us by storm. By this time the weather improved and the sun came out. Things seemed like a normal Sunday, except within our own building.

'I, along with the police, started to list bodies as far as we could with a view to identification. This was almost impossible in many cases because the bodies were so badly charred that it was difficult to tell what sex they were. One of the most awful experiences I had with regard to the victims, was a family - a father, mother and two children, and to me it seemed so tragic that they were so near to the airport and yet this disaster had befallen them.

'The day went on and we discussed whether or not we should have a service, but within the other hall we did hold a short service in the evening, with prayers for those lying injured in hospital.

'During the following week I was given time off from Stockport College, where I worked, to help with counselling relatives who came to Stockport. The police in this instance were very helpful. Salvation Army officers from Manchester arrived, and one stayed with us all week giving what help he could.

'To my mind it was the worst weekend that we had experienced in the Salvation Army in Stockport in all the years I had been in attendance, and that dates back all my life. I had seen battle - I landed in Normandy on D-Day. I was a Commander of a Crusader tank attached to the Royal Artillery and went all the way through the campaign to Lubeck on the Baltic. Prior to that I had been called as a witness to the camp at Belsen, where of course 40,000 bodies had been found. I was there on the second day the camp had been discovered and to my mind this tragedy on our own doorstep was something akin to what I had seen over there in action.'

Arthur was to receive a further shock later that day. He says, 'People were coming along with children and asking at the door of the Citadel - "Can we have a look at the bodies?" We turned them away of course, obviously. It was a peep show as far as some were concerned. I couldn't believe what I actually saw.'

Bertha Thorniley, Arthur's wife and Salvation Army member, has her own memories of that day. 'I arrived at the Citadel a short time after the crash. I saw a gentleman on Hillgate with a child on his shoulders, he said to me, "There's a plane come down in Waterloo." I came into the building and realised there were children about who had come for Sunday School. We got them into the senior place and settled them down because by this time news had filtered through as to what had exactly happened and what our bandsmen were doing. Somebody said, "we're going to need some food", so I set off for home and eventually got in touch with Mr Clayton who opened his shop and gave us what he could. When I was driving home the roads were clear, but when I came back I had an awful job to get through because of the crowds.

'I don't know what I was prepared for really, but thinking back I didn't feel anything at all. I just realised there were things we had to do. The only people I can remember being there were Arthur - who was not my husband at the time - and my sister-in-law. I just looked at these bodies and realised there were various parts missing, because at this time they had not been covered up, and we were still trying to identify them. We just tried to put people together.

Emergency services were hampered by the vast crowd of onlookers (Stockport Express)

It was amazing really. We carried on doing what we had to do, we didn't stop to eat, we never thought about it. At the end of the room on the raised platform there was what I can only describe as 'tree trunks' - they were the people we were never going to identify. Even then there was no feeling whatsoever, it was as if it wasn't happening. It was the strangest, strangest of feelings. There were quite a number of bodies that were whole. I remember one little boy he just had some dust on his face as if nothing had happened. There were several like that.

'Later we came into the main building - still with this numb feeling - and had a short service before going home.'

Sergeant Charles Hunt was at home when he heard the news on the radio. He quickly changed into his uniform and set off to drive to the town centre, holding his helmet out of the window as he went to get through the traffic. 'I left my car outside the police station and went in. I was told to go across to open the mortuary at the Stockport Sunday School where some bodies had been taken. I had a small team of constables and a doctor and some nurses who had come over from the infirmary. At first we tried to separate the bodies

Rescuers sift through the wreckage in the vain hope of finding someone still alive   (Stockport Express)

into males and females but it wasn't always possible as they were in a terrible fragile state. There was certainly no possibility of recognising anyone facially apart from about four or five people, one aircrew and girl of about six without a mark on her. There were one or two more like that, perhaps about five in all.

'One thing I do remember about that day, was a man with two young children about eight or ten. He was reasonably well dressed, he spoke well, in other words he wasn't a 'scruff'. He said to me, "Can I bring the children in to see the bodies?" He was quickly sent on his way.

'We were half anticipating that there would be more dead coming from the infirmary because the situation was fluid then. We knew we had 32 bodies but we didn't know what was at the Citadel, but we knew if there were more bodies to come they would be coming to us, so we had to keep the road clear. A man drove up, he wanted to park his car outside because he had brought his children to see the crash. I told him we were waiting for ambulances, he said, "I don't care, I want to park here, it's a street, I can park in it if I want." The ground was a bit rough, it hadn't been developed and there was a 20 foot ditch. I said, park your car there and it will be down that ditch when you get back. Off he went to complain. I saw him go up the steps into the police station and thirty seconds later he came out with a boot behind him.

Stockport Sunday School - one of the temporary mortuaries

'It was things like that, that stick in your mind. But what sticks in my mind most is the help. That's the primary thing I remember, people didn't have to help. If you're a uniformed organisation you've got to help, no question, but there were those who didn't have to. I will always remember that.'

Into the bustle and clamour of Manchester Airport death intruded suddenly. Some fifty relatives and friends were waiting to greet parents, brothers, sisters and children. For them, the first inkling that something was wrong came with a matter-of-fact announcement that flight BD542 from Palma, due to arrive at 9:20am, would be 40 minutes late. Ten o'clock came and passed. Out on the runway the Airport Fire Service stood in readiness for what was believed to be an emergency landing.

As time passed the concern grew. Then, another announcement asked them all to go to a private lounge. Once assembled in the suite of rooms the Airport Director, George Harvey, who had been summoned from home, entered and broke the news of the disaster.

(P. Hodgson)

(P. Hodgson)

Then came the grief. Pandemonium broke out, women fainted, others wept, while airport staff, near to tears themselves tried to comfort them. Nurses took care of those in a state of deep shock, brandy was dispensed and blankets wrapped around the shoulders of shivering and sobbing women. Puzzled children asked unanswerable questions. It was an impossible task.

Now began the long wait until the casualty lists could confirm who had survived.

Three long hours later the British Midland Airways station manager, Michael Bishop, entered the room now thick with cigarette smoke, and read out a list of twelve names - the names of those twelve taken out of the aircraft alive. For a handful it came as blessed relief - but for the majority of those waiting it snuffed out the last spark of hope.

Just outside the door the bustle of airport life went on; the whine of the aircraft engines, the flight announcements over the tannoy and the happy chatter of holidaymakers ... Life went on - and that was probably the hardest thing of all to bear.

Melvyn Scorah was at his home in Clitheroe, when he received a telephone call.

'I remember it being quite a nice morning. Whilst my wife Joan was getting ready for church, I went into the garden with my coffee and the Sunday paper. The telephone rang and I dashed back in. It was Arthur Werrett, Vivienne's dad (my brother-in-law) phoning from the airport to say there had been a crash. They were, as I understood it 'locked in' a VIP lounge, that is to say not allowed to go out, because at that stage they didn't know about survivors or anything, and I think in panic he phoned me to go over and see if I could help. I informed my wife Joan of this, and we climbed into the car and immediately set out for the airport. In those days there were no motorways as such and the airport was a nightmare to get to. Basically it involved going through all the towns and villages between Clitheroe and Manchester for a start, and from that point out towards the airport.

'On the way we had the car radio on picking up what information we could, not really knowing what we could do, apart from being a prop and a help, because understandably they were going to be terribly upset. Then, as we were going through Manchester town centre and I was looking to strike out towards the airport, a news bulletin came on the radio - and it always stuck in my mind because it changed the course of our direction - the reporter said he had just walked away from the crash site, and all that could be seen was smoking wreckage and the relatives being led away. We put two and two together and decided they were no longer at the airport. They must have been taken to Stockport, and without thinking how we were going to find them, set off directly to the town centre.

'Along the way we were stopped a couple of times at police road blocks which were diverting traffic away from Stockport. We just gave the information that we had a relative on the plane and we were flagged through. Coming into the town centre we spotted signs for the police station and headed there, again stopped by a policeman who directed us into the car park.

'We went into the police station and were taken upstairs. It was set up like an incident room, people all over the place, benches, tables, files, telephones and everything going on. We were taken on one side and interviewed as to who we were and who we had on the plane, which was obviously Vivienne, my niece and her friend Susan. We were told there were some survivors but had no lists. That's as much as they could tell us, but could we leave a telephone number where we could be contacted. My mother and father lived in Nelson in those days, so I gave them my parents number knowing there would be somebody there to receive messages.

'We then came out of the police station not knowing what to do for the best. I said, let's go and see if we can get nearer the scene. There might be an incident van there that can give us a bit more information. We walked down and there were crowds and crowds of people. I managed to get near enough - my wife wouldn't come further than the particular corner she was standing on - I went towards the scene and went up on tiptoe and looked over the tops of people. All I could see was this great big aeroplane tail-fin stuck up in the air and nothing else. Everywhere was charred burnt wreckage, smoke still rising from it. I just walked away and said to Joan, there's nobody come out of that alive. At that point we felt so desperately low, and again, not knowing what to do we wandered aimlessly down the road, with no purpose in mind, just trying to collect our thoughts. By accident we came across the Salvation Army Citadel, and I wondered if they had any information. I spoke to a lady in the doorway. She took all my details down, as had the police, again with the telephone number for Nelson. She apologised, saying that at that time they hadn't enough details to release any names.

'With that we wandered away up the street discussing things as we went along. We had now twice given my mother's telephone number. I thought we should find a telephone box, phone home and let them know of the possibility of someone phoning with news. At the top of the rise there was a telephone box, so I went in and called home. It was my brother who answered. He had gone up to be with my parents. He said, "Have you heard anything?" I said, No, that's why I'm phoning. He said, "Before you go any further, the Salvation Army have phoned, she's alive, and so is her friend. They're both in Stockport Infirmary." At which point I broke down.

'My wife carried on speaking on the phone. I went out of the box and I saw a man walking down the street and asked him where Stockport Infirmary was - in fact we were by the door! The phone box was virtually set up to the wall of the building. My wife joined me and we went through a doorway into a big waiting room with bench seats, but what was strange - it was totally empty. There wasn't a soul about, only a lady at the reception desk. I explained who we were, she told us to take a seat and she disappeared. After waiting about five minutes, a gentleman appeared - who I found out later was the Police Chaplain, Arthur Connop. He sat down and went through all the details of who we were and what relatives we had on board - we also explained about Vivienne's friend Susan as well. He turned and looked at his clipboard and said, "Yes, they are both alive, would you like to see them?"

'We were then taken upstairs to a ward where all the survivors were. We were the first relatives in there. We found that quite a moving experience. The sheer emotion of that I have always found difficult to explain. Within about an hour we had gone through hell, come back out and gone back in again, and finally we were face to face with the fact that she had survived.

'We sat with Vivienne for some time. She was conscious and able to tell us bits. She remembered looking out and thinking they were rather low over the house tops. She then drifted off again. I think she was sedated a little at that stage. I walked across with Joan and sat with Susan for a while. About fifteen minutes later all the rest of the relatives arrived from the airport, including Vivienne's parents, Joan and Arthur.

'We were allocated a room across from the ward, which we could use as a lounge. We were warned not to go outside the hospital through the main doors because the press were there. The doctor came and spoke to us regarding what he hoped to do with Vivienne's badly broken leg, but he had grave doubts at that stage as to whether he could save it.

'Sometime later, when she was wheeled back from surgery, we were standing in the doorway, my sister Joan - not to be confused with Joan my wife - turned round and said to me, "I can't go near, will you go and tell me if her leg is still there?" I followed the trolley down into the ward. They put her into

Starboard wing embedded in the back wall of the sub-station (Barrie Dean)

A mobile crane moves Hotel Golf's tail section (Barrie Dean)

the bed and I went over and lifted the sheets, and I saw two legs - it was quite comical in a way.

'That day was a shattering experience for me, and one I will never forget.'

At first there was only a handful of spectators, but as news of the disaster was broadcast over the radio and TV, thousands flocked to the scene, to the detriment of the rescue and assisting services. Cars were parked indiscriminately, many three abreast, and the main roads leading to the crash were jammed with pedestrians and motorists. Traffic jams surpassed that of a Friday evening rush hour, and a large number of police, who could have been used more effectively elsewhere, had to be diverted to control them.

The crowds clustered round to see the helpless victims being carried away. Others craned their necks to see the scene of devastation. Parents held up small children above the crowd for a better look. Then there were arguments with the police because they refused to let them get closer. As time went on swarms of people travelling on all kinds of vehicles were asking, "Which way to the crash?" Groups of youths climbed on rooftops to get an advantage over others. Many forced their way through the police cordon, and at one time twenty people were standing on the sagging roof of a derelict house.

Brian Donohoe remembers returning home that evening to his baker's shop in Hillgate:

'All of Stockport was a bottleneck, but in Hillgate there were thousands, thousands of people. It was like coming out of the Wembley Cup Final - ice-cream carts, hot dog sellers and we even had a couple with a picnic table set up on the pavement eating sandwiches.'

These appalling scenes were no doubt due to the news announcements, the novelty of air crashes and the fact that Sunday was a workless day. One senior police officer said that he had never witnessed such careless behaviour in the whole of his service. Even eight hours later the streets within half a mile of the crash were still thronged with cars and pedestrians, and this situation, to a somewhat lesser degree persisted for several days. It was for many a grotesque carnival.

Chris McNeill, a member of the Red Cross, Cheadle Detachment, drove into Stockport and was horrified at the sight that greeted her. She had received a telephone call at home from her Commandant, informing her of the crash and telling her to go to one of the temporary mortuaries.

'All the roads were blocked and ice-cream vendors had moved quickly into the area to sell their wares to the ghouls who had come to stare and gawp at the scene. Eventually I broke through the crowds - my uniform helped - and reached the hall. The whole floor area was covered with corpses and a terrible acrid smell of burnt flesh filled the air. It was truly an appalling sight and one which I will never forget. The smell pervaded the room and got right into one's nostrils. Cans and cans of 'Haze' air freshener were sprayed everywhere. I have never bought 'Haze' from that day - I am sure certain smells provoke certain memories and that is one memory I want to forget.'

David Hamilton, who reported the news that day for ITN, clearly remembers this aspect of the disaster. Thirty years on he recalls those events.

'The Sunday morning peace at our Marple bungalow was shattered by a phone call from Dougie Fairbairn at the Didsbury studios. He told me to get dressed and get to the centre of Stockport immediately. A plane has crashed in the town. We're sending a unit and we want you to report on it for ITN.

David Hamilton

'It took Dougie, a man with a reputation as a joker, a lot of persuasion before I realised he was serious and I roared off to Stockport. When I arrived at the scene, the chaos and devastation were unbelievable. The pilot had managed to miss every house and the plane had crumpled up on some open land. A few yards away in any direction and the result would have been even more devastating. Pieces of aircraft were strewn around and as rescue workers sorted the injured from the dead and carried them away on stretchers I fed the news to ITN for their lunchtime bulletin.

'To somebody like myself who had never before come close to any sort of disaster, the scene was shattering, but it became even more sickening as news of it spread. Hundreds of people came to gape at the appalling destruction and loss of life, and with them came ice-cream and hot dog sellers, setting up their pitches. It was like a carnival, a carnival with human misery as the main attraction.

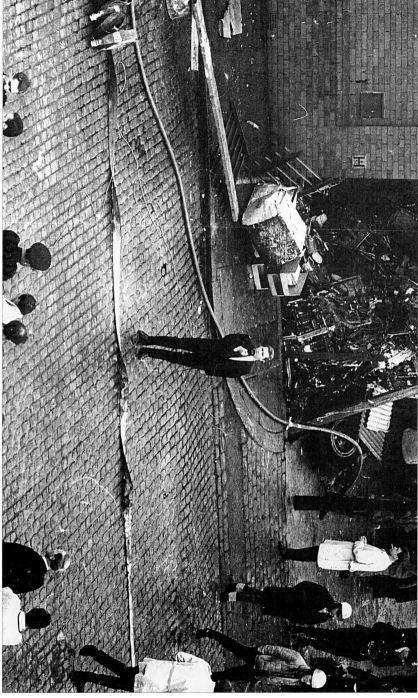

(David Hamilton)

40

'But having to report on it was an example of the sort of versatility that TV called for in those days. Royston Mayoh, who directed that outside broadcast from Stockport, had been in the studio the night before directing 'Opportunity Knocks', and the last time I'd been seen on national TV was in a knockabout sketch with Ken Dodd. Both of us had to forget our entertainment backgrounds for that tragic and harrowing day.'

Another reporter in the thick of it that day was Bob Greaves of Granada TV. Here he describes how the day's events unfolded:

'There are some days you are never likely to forget, and the day of the Stockport disaster is one of them. I was at home in Sale - at the time I was Granada's News Editor and fledgling news reader - when I received a phone call from a contact in the Manchester police force telling me there had been an air crash in Stockport. It was within minutes of the event, and the message was a touch garbled and lacked detail. I made a few quick calls myself to try to assess the strength of the story, which may sound callous, but has to be done by journalists. I soon realised that it was a major disaster, so I called my departmental boss, David Plowright, at his home in Cheshire.

'Once I had convinced him it was a serious crash, he and I started to 'round up' technicians and journalists, who of course were not in the office or

(P. Hodgson)

41

studios. In those days there were no scheduled weekend news bulletins, and indeed, Granada did not really exist at weekends. Its licence was to transmit programmes throughout the North West and Yorkshire, because ABC Television, based in Didsbury were the weekend company. They did not have a full news-desk operation, so it was really down to us, plus some of their staff, to get on with what proved to be a harrowing day's work.

'I recollect that our reporting team included Alan Towers, and possibly Bill Grundy, though once I had finished my organising people from home, I and others joined our teams in Stockport, and we all played our part in the operation, finding out background and doing interviews with witnesses and the emergency services. ITN in London did not have a regional office or staff in the north in those days, so we fed a whole lot of live and recorded material to them for transmission throughout the British Isles.

Bob Greaves

'One particular memory I do have is that within an hour or so of the crash, the police were asking us to put an appeal out on the air trying to persuade people not to go into the town centre of Stockport. Because the crash had happened in such an accessible area, ice-cream vans and various food vendors had made their way there, as well as thousands trying to catch glimpses of the crash site, and the activity going on. Human nature, I suppose - rather like the modern-day equivalent of motorists slowing down on motorways when accidents happen to 'rubberneck' what is going on.

'I like to think that our day's work was done without intrusion, and with the humanity that good journalists can demonstrate in what can be very difficult conditions.'

The Reverend Arthur Connop, Chaplain to the police, fire and ambulance services and also Stockport Infirmary, was in the vestry at Tiviot Dale Methodist Church, waiting to go into the pulpit.

'I got a call at the church to say there had been an incident and would I attend. I had no idea what had happened. I thought I was on my way to a road accident.'

Arriving at the scene, he wandered around the wreckage, trying, like so many others, to help those who were beyond help.

'Debris - that was all. The scene was both pitiful and shocking. People were rushing to help and the fire crews were fighting the blaze. It was incredible how everyone just pulled together and became a team. I realised there was little I could do on the scene, the others could do this kind of thing far better than me. A Senior Police Officer asked me to go to the infirmary to make arrangements for meeting relatives as they arrived.

'We had expected that all the relatives would rush to Stockport. We didn't know that the radio had told them to go to the airport. This gave us some breathing space. Eventually, of course, the relatives began to arrive here. By that time we had prepared a room. I do remember the first couple to arrive was a young man and woman. The man was asking about his mother, father and sister, and the young lady was asking about her sister who was travelling with them.

'People were terribly upset. One minute they were waiting to welcome home their relatives and friends and the next minute their loved ones were dead and gone. I did what I could, but it isn't easy to comfort people in that situation. How can you comfort relatives? I think, here is a mother, a father, a child, a somebody. I can't think in terms of multiple casualties, there is little to say, religious or any other kind of talk. All you can do is be kind, compassionate, so that you feel what they feel.' Arthur's home was open to relatives and helpers. Alice, his wife, provided hospitality, support and comfort in addition to visiting the survivors in hospital, where she especially remembers the Wood boys with whom she sat and played.

For the next week, Arthur spent his time between the Infirmary and the police station. It was his grim duty to inform many of the relatives of the loss of their loved ones. It was, however, a more pleasing task to comfort those who had come through the ordeal alive.

Arthur was upset that the newspapers had made him out to be a hero, without even talking to him.

'I wasn't heroic. Few people involved were. It fell to us to do what we could, and we did it as best we could.'

By mid-day five extra telephone lines had been provided at Police Headquarters, where an emergency control room was set up. This was under the supervision of a senior officer with a mixed staff of police and civilians. Their duty was to log and deal with all messages connected with the accident.

In the early stages every line was fully occupied by enquiries from relatives, many of whom had been waiting at the airport, and from the media. To prevent repeated press enquiries, it was announced that two press conferences would be held at 4pm and 10pm, and would be addressed by the Chief Constable, Leonard Massey. The control room dealt not only with the Accident Investigation Branch of the Board of Trade, witnesses, medical and dental reports, but with a wide range of other questions. The early establishment of this room prevented what otherwise would have been an impossible overloading of the normal communications system.

By 12:30 all the bodies had been recovered. A second mortuary had now been set up in the Sunday School at the nearby Centenary Hall. In order to ensure that a complete search could be made of the wreckage, sections of the aircraft were moved by mobile cranes to more convenient positions. The rescue workers, their faces and hands blackened by smoke, some with blood stained shirts, toiled at the scene, pausing only to accept mugs of tea from Salvation Army and WRVS members who had set up emergency canteens. They continued to sift through the debris for anything that might lead to the

Rescuers stand clear as part of the wreckage is hoisted away   (Stockport Express)

identity of the unknown victims lying in the two temporary mortuaries. One rescue worker from a nearby factory, who toiled for three hours at the scene pleaded with a reporter after being interviewed, 'Please do not publish my name, I couldn't bear having my friends ask me for more details.' While this work went on aircraft continued to fly over the scene on their way to Manchester Airport.

Almost without exception, suitcases, hand luggage and documents were destroyed by fire, although a few passports and other means of identity were recovered from bodies and clothing. Where possible, jewellery was recorded and left on the body until pathological examination was carried out.

In each of the two temporary mortuaries a senior police officer was put in charge. Ante rooms were prepared for identification purposes and chaplains were made available to comfort relatives who came to identify their next of kin. Identification by relatives was delayed as long as possible in order to clean and arrange bodies - some of which presented a frightening spectacle - and to ensure corroborative evidence from dental and medical sources. A casualty Officer from the hospital was attached to each mortuary and in every case life was pronounced extinct. Bodies were divided into groups for identification, males, females and children, so as to prevent inspection of unnecessary large numbers by the next of kin.

Wreckage is piled by the roadside   (Barrie Dean)

It quickly became evident that a special procedure was necessary to deal with the problems of relatives and friends of the casualties now arriving at Police Headquarters in considerable numbers. It was decided to set up in a large hall, charts showing the disposition and details of all victims, the correlation of the property to the passengers, a progress chart showing how far visual, dental, medical and pathological methods of identification had progressed, and other miscellaneous information relative to each individual casualty. This room also housed police officers to interview and help relatives and friends. Arthur Connop, the Police Chaplain, with other ministers assisted, refreshments were provided and everything possible was done to comfort and help the bereaved.

The securing of the passenger list was vital before relatives could be contacted. The usual practice was for one copy to be carried on the aircraft - which in this case was destroyed in the fire - and one copy to be retained at the point of departure. As this was Palma, with whom communications were notoriously bad, it wasn't until 11:30 on the night of the disaster before a complete list was telexed through to Stockport. There was a passenger list available of those who flew out at the start of the holiday, but this could not be relied on as correct for the return journey.

Jacky Martinez, who was employed by Arrowsmiths Holidays running their Palma office, was given the task of compiling that list of passengers she had been with only hours earlier.

'My job was to arrange accommodation, excursions and transfers. From time to time I was asked to do the odd weekend transfer, which is exactly what I did on the Saturday night, 3 June 1967.

'At the time of the disaster I was based at the Tahiti Hotel in Palma Nova, so I got to know the clients quite well. Some groups are awful, some OK and some very nice, this was one of the better ones. In particular there was a gay couple, and one of them played the piano in the bar for a sing song most nights - he was great. Another couple had a daughter about eight years old, who sang into the microphone on the coach coming back from the barbecue and was a real entertainer. There was also another couple I remember with two teenage children. They were late for the transfer coach back to the airport. We were just about to leave when they just came strolling along! I think all of the above perished.

'I had planned to fly home that weekend as my gran was ill and it was mum's birthday. We had two flights back to Manchester - the British Midland and a Caledonian. My boss's wife had just given birth in the UK so he took the only remaining seat which was on the Caledonian aircraft, so I couldn't go. I sent a telegram to my mum to tell her I couldn't make it and to wish her a happy birthday for the 4 June! She had just heard the news on the radio about the crash when the telegram arrived and she thought it was to tell her that I was on board.

'If I remember correctly the flight was delayed, but I can't remember why or for how long. I did the transfer from the Palma Nova - Magaluf side, and one of the other reps did the Arenal - C'an Pastilla. It was late when I got back to Palma Nova.

'About lunch time on the Sunday, the receptionist from the Tahiti came banging on my door to tell me that Arrowsmiths were holding on the phone and that I had to go immediately. I was given the terrible news and had to contact the head rep, Mel Rossello. I had to go with Mel to see the parents of one of the survivors - Susan Howarth - who were staying at the Hotel El Cid in C'an Pastilla. We arranged for them to fly back to the UK the same day.

'On the Monday morning when I went to open the office at 8:45 there were approximately twenty clients waiting outside. They had heard the news by this time and were refusing to return home on the Argonaut. Some of them were quite nasty and threatening. In the end the Argonaut was never used by Arrowsmiths again, the rest of the seasons flights were operated by Laker Airways One-eleven jets.'

As the day drew to a close and the light faded over Stockport, those men and women who had toiled for hours at the disaster scene simply drifted away wearily. They could do no more.

A policeman's grim expression epitomises the hopelessness
of finding more survivors

(Stockport Express)

Chapter Four

VICTIMS

As Monday dawned over Stockport, the town tried to come to terms and make sense of this dreadful disaster that had befallen them. At the crash site the wreckage had been gathered into three major piles, two from the aircraft and another made up of cars and vans destroyed in the garage. The huge tail made up a fourth section. Board of Trade accident investigators moved a caravan into Hopes Carr as a mobile base. They would work at the site for a week examining the wreckage for clues, and supervise the loading of some fifty tons of aircraft components onto RAF Queen Mary trailers to be transported by road to the Royal Aircraft Establishment, Farnborough.

Early on Monday morning a conference was held at Police Headquarters between the Chief Constable, the two RAF pathologists, senior police officers and the Coroner. The Coroner agreed to open the inquest and also to hold an Inquest every evening until all the bodies had been dealt with, so as not to delay the issuing of burial certificates.

Wreckage being loaded onto Queen Mary trailers for transportation to Farnborough (Brian Robinson)

49

As the day progressed the full extent of the tragedy began to unfold as the names of those killed were released.

Amongst local victims were Catherine (Katie) Brooks 63, her friends Eliza and James Booth - who lived less than a mile from where the aircraft crashed - and Dorothy Ackroyd aged 73. All were members of the Gorsey Bank Bowling Club, who had made up a foursome for the holiday.

John Benton from Bramhall put off his holiday with his family and stayed at home to study for exams he was due to take. On the Sunday morning he left his parents home in his father's car to meet them at the airport. It was there he learned of the crash in which his father, mother, and 15 year old sister Christine died. The fourth member of the party, Christine's friend, Fiona Child survived.

Other victims from Stockport were Brian and Ann Stott, who ran the Stockport Road post office in Cheadle. They had left their two children - Philip, aged 3 and Mandy, aged 7, at home with relatives.

Jean Walsh, 39, died with her husband, Thomas, 41, and their two children, William, 6, and Jeanette, 5. Mrs Walsh owned a chemist's shop in Middleton, near Manchester, and was at the time the only woman member of the Pharmaceutical Society of England. Her husband worked in the pathology laboratory at Booth Hall Children's Hospital.

Ever since she was a child, Lillian Nolan from Middleton, had a deep-rooted fear of being 33 - the age at which her mother died. She was killed along with her 10 year old daughter, Julia - she was just 33! Her husband, Jack, was waiting at Manchester Airport with a welcome home present. He also lost his sister, Glenise and his brother-in-law, Alex, in the crash.·The four had booked originally with another company, but the tour was cancelled because there were insufficient bookings, so at the last minute they took the holiday to Majorca instead.

From Manchester was television writer Harry Stansfield, who wrote comedy sketches for the 'Jimmy Clitheroe Show'. His wife, Joan, aged 38, and their 10 year old son, John, also died.

From Salford, was Arthur Kemp, a television engineer, and his wife, Elsie. They were returning from their annual holiday. Both were in their late fifties and left two sons.

A youngster examines the wreckage   (Brian Robinson)

For Blackpool couple, Alan Hughes and his wife, Kathleen, it was their first holiday abroad together. They left their two children, Marshall, aged 8, and Allison, aged 5, at home with Mrs Hughes' mother.

Damaged buildings on Waterloo Road (Brian Robinson)

Among the dead were Bernard Dowd and his wife Jane from Chester. Mr Dowd was in his late fifties and was headmaster of St. Bede's Roman Catholic School. He had planned to retire on health grounds when he reached sixty. Ironically, the couple lived only a few minutes walk away from Mr and Mrs Bray who lost their lives in the Air Ferry DC-4 which crashed in Perpignan, twelve hours earlier.

Many of the victims came from Yorkshire, like Ronald and Annie Cowgill, from Wibsey, Bradford. Their deaths orphaned three boys, aged 9, 13 and 15.

Three members of a Selby family died, leaving two girls, aged 19 and 15. They were Philip Thorne, a market gardener, his wife Jean and their 12 year old son Peter, who was a boarder at Skipton Grammar School. Their daughters who did not make the trip were Susan who was studying at Leeds University and Helen.

A devoted couple who lived for today - that was how stunned neighbours and friends described Roy and Margaret Latham from Sheffield. Many of them had received post cards only a few days earlier telling them of the 'wonderful' holiday they were having. The Lathams had gone on holiday with Michael and Janet Ayland who also died.

There were no survivors from the Shaw family from Leeds. Edward Shaw, his wife Gloria and their 9 year old twins, Jeremy and Maxine, died, together with Gloria's parents, Arthur and Ethel Reynolds.

Widow, Elsie James, aged 51 from Wombwell, was a reluctant holidaymaker who did not want to fly. She had made earlier flights including one to Rome but this time had a strange premonition. She told her sister before she left about this feeling, but her sister dismissed it, pointing out that the risks of road and rail travel were far greater. Her friend and neighbour, Sheila Glass, said, 'She sent many letters and postcards telling us what a wonderful holiday she was having. The weather had been perfect and the only thing she missed was seeing my children and her own friends. The last card we had from her ended, "See you at Manchester at nine o'clock Sunday morning."' Elsie James died with her friend Alice Godwin from Ossett.

Little 12 year old Ann Tomlinson had spent a dream holiday splashing around while learning to swim in the warm waters of the Mediterranean before disaster struck. She died with her parents and 16 year old brother Michael. They came from Clowne, Derbyshire. Her father, Raymond Tomlinson had served in the RAF during the war and was a member of Sheffield Flying Club at Netherthorpe where he was a keen pilot.

A full list of all those killed in the disaster appears in appendix II

On the Monday morning Bertha Thorniley returned to the Hillgate Citadel to help with the grieving relatives.

'At the time I worked as an auxiliary at Stepping Hill Hospital. I went and spoke to the Matron and she gave me the Monday off to go back to the Citadel to help with the identification.

'I remember this lady holding my arm, she said, "You will know my daughter, she was wearing a reversible coat." It hit me then. It really did hit me that there had been this terrible tragedy, and what we had been attending were actual people not just bodies. It then began to tell on me. That lady was so sure that I would know her daughter because of this reversible coat. I knew I couldn't help this lady, because there could be no reversible coat, everything had been destroyed in the fire.

'Then other relatives came. One lady said to me, "They had everything to come back to." I had no answer to that either. But not one of those relatives who spoke to me asked why, which is a normal reaction isn't it, to ask why has this happened to me? It was as if everybody was in a daze and it wasn't happening to them either, and I should imagine that as the days went on they would get the same reaction as I got on that second day. It was the strangest experience I've ever had.'

Most of the police officers who were actually engaged in removing the passengers from the aircraft were affected to some degree by shock, amnesia and a prolonged sense of frustration. Two of the officers who were at the centre of the rescue operations, experienced a deep sense of frustration at having had to watch passengers who were appealing for help, burn to death because of the utter impossibility of further approach. One officer, a week later, could not remember what sort of rescue operations he had undertaken. Another officer absented himself from duty three days after the event without any given reason, and at a later stage, whilst still on duty, had to be taken home.

At the scene, policemen and others who had been unable to rescue further passengers and had been confronted with a child and others who could not be rescued because of the fire, simply sat down dejectedly and wept.

It was clear that the disposal of 72 bodies would take a week at least and that in the warm weather decomposition would occur rapidly. Efforts were made to provide refrigeration facilities. Stockport had suitable plants but they were either in use for food storage or had other limitations. Manchester had nothing that was ideally suitable for body preservation. Though they had deep freezing plants the temperatures were too low for subsequent post-mortem work. In the end it became necessary to obtain three large insulated containers refrigerated by dry ice. These were put into use on the day following the crash.

Identification was the greatest problem and was based on five methods - visual identification by next of kin, personal possessions, jewellery etc., dental, medical and pathological examination.

Visual identification by relatives was of very little use, due to the gross disfigurement by burning. In several cases this method resulted in wrong identification. Dental identification proved to be very valuable and dental histories were sought in every possible case. In addition a dental expert from Guy's Hospital assisted the pathologists in their post-mortem examinations. In the end pathological and dental examination was able to accurately determine the identification of every one of the 72 bodies.

A team of twelve worked on the post-mortems and every examination was carefully recorded. The last body was handed over for burial on the twelfth day after the disaster.

The death toll of 72 at Stockport came just twelve hours after another British airliner crashed in the Pyrenees, killing 88. With a total of 160 dead in both accidents it was the blackest weekend in British civil aviation history. But behind each of those victims were the other victims, the relatives and friends left to grieve.

Early in 1998 I began tracing the relatives of those killed so they could have the opportunity to attend the memorial unveiling and service which was

Pathology team - Police Coroners Officer Roger Gaskell (3rd from left); Centre: Group Captain Mason; Sqd Leader Tarlton

(Roger Gaskell)

56

scheduled to take place in the June. Besides spending many hours on the telephone chasing up leads, I published a number of newspaper appeals in the areas where the victims came from, asking the relatives to contact me.

I would like to relate here the story of two sisters, Pauline O'Sullivan and Marilyn Bradley. They lost not only their parents but also their brother David and cousin Philip Cruse. At the time of the disaster they lived in Slaithwaite, Yorkshire.

Their parents, Arthur and Rachel Smith were married in 1937 in Wolverhampton. In 1939, when war broke out Arthur Smith was posted to Egypt. Arthur and Rachel kept in touch by writing to each other almost every day for six years. When the war was over Arthur returned to Wolverhampton where he got a job in confectionery sales. In the winter of 1945-46 they moved to Newcastle upon Tyne. Soon afterwards Pauline was born, followed by Marilyn in 1950 and their son David in 1952. Rachel's sister Janet also moved to Newcastle where she married John Cruse, who was

Rachel and Arthur Smith   (Pauline O'Sullivan)

blinded during the war serving in the RAF. They had a son, Philip and a daughter Rosalyn.

Pauline and Marilyn take up the story.

'Dad was a great organiser of events, like car rallies, treasure hunts, bonfire parties, Sunday School outings, quizzes, hikes etc. We remember a lot of fun things he did. After moving to Huddersfield, in 1959 he eventually became Sales Director for Rileys, Nuttalls and Callard and Bowser confectionery. He ran the Sunday School as Superintendent and preached in churches around West Yorkshire, even though most of the time he was in pain with a rare form of arthritis (one of the reasons for going on holiday abroad was to benefit from the sun). Mum did the shopping for the 'old dears' in the village and visited them regularly to make sure they were eating properly and keeping warm and well. She enjoyed attending classes, cooking and making a cosy home for her family. We had a very close happy family life and lovely holidays together.

'Our brother, David, was always interested in aircraft, and said he wanted to be a test pilot one day. Our cousin, Philip, was about to take his GCE 'O' Levels. He used to cycle all over on his bike. Unfortunately, he had always been accident prone - wherever he went something happened. One of the things we remember just before they set off was that we were all joking about Philip being on the same plane ...'

Pauline's daughter, Rachel, was born on what would have been Philip's 20th birthday if he had lived. It was Rachel who travelled from Yorkshire to Manchester to visit friends on the 23 January 1998 (which was also Marilyn's birthday) and read about plans for the memorial in a Manchester newspaper and passed this on to her mother.

Soon after I made contact with Pauline, she told me how she heard the tragic news that day, and how life would never be the same again.

'Sunday 4 June 1967 is a day I will never forget. I remember getting out of bed and pulling back the curtains. I looked up at the sky and thought, they will be landing any time now.

'I had just started preparing lunch for the family when the phone rang - mum said she would phone from the airport when they landed. It was John Barlow - a colleague of Dad's - he needed to know details. He said that he didn't want to alarm us, but there had been an air crash near to Manchester. I just couldn't believe what I was hearing. He said he would come over to the house straightaway. The phone rang again - perhaps this is Mum I thought, hopefully - it was in fact my boyfriend Ted, just checking if everything was alright. He was convinced there was a mix-up as there had been another holiday air crash the previous day over France. Anyway, he and his cousin Sean said they would come over straight away.

'Ted and I were engaged and Mum and Dad said they would bring us a present from Majorca. Marilyn stayed at home as she had a horse and was entering a show with him.

Cousin Philip   (Pauline O'Sullivan)

'Soon after, the phone rang again, by now I knew that something was definitely wrong. It was Auntie Janet - Philip's Mum - checking if they had

Brother David   (Pauline O'Sullivan)

arrived home safely. I tried so hard to stay calm and just said that they must have been delayed. She was chatting about my 21st birthday which was to be the following month. I felt sick and trembling, but I didn't want to tell her my fears at that stage.

'Ted, Sean and John Barlow all arrived within minutes and we all waited. We turned the TV news on and that was when the horror became real, for most of the news was about the air crash. Marilyn wanted to go to the scene straightaway, but everyone was advised to keep away. It all seemed like a nightmare and any minute I would wake up and everything would be alright. This feeling lasted a long, long time - weeks or even months. We did not actually receive confirmation from the police until the following day.

'The following week the funeral took place. The sight of the four coffins beside each other was almost too much to bear. The little Chapel at the cemetery in Slaithwaite was packed. Philip had been buried with Mum, Dad and David.

'After returning home we knew nothing would ever be the same again but we were young and life had to go on. In those days there was no counselling; you just had to get on with it on your own. But there was more heartache to follow, as our grandparents never got over the shock. Grandad Smith died in November that year and Gran Smith died the following May. We had lost six of our loved ones within twelve months. Before the 4 June 1967 I hadn't been to a funeral ever.

'Ted and I married in 1968. We have two children, Rachel and Tim, and we are a very close loving family. Every year I stay with Auntie Janet in Newcastle and visit Rosalyn - Philip's sister - and her family. We still talk of the happy times before that dreadful day.'

Marilyn, like her sister, still vividly recalls the horror of that day.

'On Sunday the 4 June 1967,' she says, 'I stood at the top of the stairs looking blindly across the fields from the large window at home. I remember thinking, this can't be happening, it only happens to 'other' people or in books. I don't know how long I stood there thinking that it was all a mistake, that of course everything would be alright. Hadn't mum and dad always made everything alright?

'I was seventeen, my sister Pauline was twenty and life was good. Why should it be anything else but good - my seventeen-year-old mind reasoned. There would be a phone call any moment saying sorry about the mistake but mum, dad, brother David and cousin Philip were on their way home for Sunday lunch.

'But it was no mistake. The plane had crashed in Stockport, so very, very close to home and safety.

'Time and events were a haze for a long, long time. We did find out that they had enjoyed their holiday and David and Philip had had fun together. Pauline and I hadn't gone on holiday as Pauline had a boyfriend and I had a horse and didn't want to miss competing in a local show. Auntie Janet had let Philip go as company for David. They had decided to take a package tour instead of the usual drive and camping holiday as it would be more restful for dad with his arthritis.

'Auntie Janet and family came for a while and we all comforted each other, and cried, and talked and cried.

'And time goes on ... and life goes on ... and now it is thirty-one years on. I have got on with life. Life does have a lot of knocks.

'Thanks mum and dad for a wonderful childhood. I'll never forget your guidance and goodness, it was that that helped us carry on. I know we will all meet again ... " above the bright blue skies" as the Sunday School song dad taught us goes.'

Pauline and Marilyn's story is personal to them, but there are many more stories that came in the aftermath of the Stockport disaster and it would require a separate volume to relate them all.

One other account I include here came to me from Helen Cuthew, who at the time was engaged to Chris Pollard the co-pilot.

Pauline O'Sullivan and Marilyn Bradley   (Pauline O'Sullivan)

'We first met when I was training to be a nurse, at the Preliminary Training School for St. Bartholomew's Hospital at Letchmore Heath, just down the road from the London School of Flying at Elstree Aerodrome where Chris was training. There was fairly lively traffic between the two places. Our first date was doing aerobatics in a school owned Chipmunk. I seem to remember that Chris was the youngest pilot to pass his Instrument Rating at that time. A good friend of Chris's owned a Piper Tripacer, which he kept at Elstree and got Chris to fly him around. In fact we all flew down to Plymouth in it to have Sunday lunch with his parents - the first time I met them. We spent a lot of time down there, in fact we got engaged there and went into Plymouth to buy the ring in the spring of 1967.

'I spoke to Chris on the phone the day before the crash and I knew he was flying that night. I was working at Gatwick Airport on the ground for the then British United Airways and as I passed the Duty Officer on the stairs he said, "Terrible news about the crash." At first I thought he was referring to the DC-4 at Perpignan, but when he said there had been another I had a dreadful premonition. It took some considerable time for him to get through to British Midland, and I remember sitting in his office while he tried to discover if it was Chris's flight. He received confirmation that it was, but there was no news as to whether Chris had survived.

'I was taken home and eventually another Duty Officer came to the house to tell me that Chris had died. British United provided a car to take me down to Cornwall to be with his parents. My parents were abroad, and I remained there until after the funeral.

'I stayed very close to his parents and continued to visit them regularly, eventually staying there with my husband and four children. They were probably the kindest people I ever met.'

On Sunday 11 June the Salvation Army held a service for the survivors at Stockport Infirmary. Arthur Thorniley wrote at the time:

'A very moving little service was held in the Infirmary Ward where a number of the survivors were lying with very severe injuries. To think exactly one week previously to the hour we had been engaged in a mission of carrying out relief to the rescued, and helping to identify those who had been suddenly taken from this world. No wonder there were many tears in the eyes of the survivors and salvationists.'

Brian Donohoe had a bad time in the wake of the disaster, he says, 'I didn't have the best of weeks. I was always told that it was the worst time they have ever seen me. I was going out delivering stuff and forgetting to bring the bread boards back ... I didn't bring anything back!'

Chapter Five

PRELUDE TO DISASTER

The real tragedy of the Stockport disaster is the fact that it need never have happened.

Abnormalities recorded in the fuel log of Hotel Golf, and a potentially dangerous fuel-related incident just one week before the Stockport crash, when Hotel Golf was on its final approach into Palma Airport, should have sounded the warning bells. But British Midland pilots and engineering staff failed to recognise these signs for what they were.

The story of Hotel Golf's violent end with the tragic loss of seventy two lives, can be directly traced back to 1953.

Correspondence between BOAC - the then operator of Hotel Golf - and Canadair, the manufacturer, shows that the airline had experienced a number of incidents involving inadvertent fuel transfer in flight.

Briefly explained, inadvertent fuel transfer is fuel transferring itself from one tank to another through an improperly closed cock, with the possibility of starving one or more engines of fuel. Fortunately for BOAC none of these incidents resulted in disaster. Aer Lingus discovered the same problem on their Carvairs, and Invicta Airlines on their DC-4s, both these aircraft having similar fuel systems to the Argonaut. After a special drive on safety, all three operators found the problem to be manageable. Provided the problem was recognised to exist, and safeguards put into place, the risk of inadvertent fuel transfer was immediately minimised.

The Public Inquiry into the Stockport accident was into its twelfth day before the above information came to light. These potentially dangerous problems involving the Argonaut's fuel system were never effectively communicated to British Midland, or other operators of the type. If the airline had been forewarned, then the disastrous emergency that overtook Hotel Golf on that wet and overcast Sunday morning, would probably not have occurred.

Argonaut Hotel Golf was manufactured in 1949 at Canadair's Dorval plant, Montreal, as construction number 153. Designated the Canadair C-4,

Hotel Golf in BOAC livery

64

it was a long range pressurised development of the Douglas DC-4, powered by four Rolls Royce Merlin engines. Hotel Golf was one of a fleet of twenty two aircraft ordered by BOAC. Given the class name Argonaut by the corporation, the aircraft entered service later that same year on its routes to Africa and the Far East.

The Argonaut as delivered was appallingly noisy. Eight stub exhausts beamed directly towards the cabin wall and windows, and the fatigue factor in the front seats, which also suffered the battering of the slipstream of the inboard propellers, which were close to the fuselage, made a very tiring flight for passengers seated in that area. Happily the crew, forward of all this commotion, did not suffer, so cheerfully went on flying without complaint. Because of the noise factor, the design engineers at Rolls Royce came up with a new manifold which took the inboard exhausts and passed them over the top of the engine to the outboard manifold. This reduced the noise to a barely tolerable level, but for the rest of its days the Argonaut was still the noisiest propliner of all. Despite this the Argonaut was favourably received by the travelling public.

Charters and special VIP flights carried the Argonaut's fame throughout the world. Charters took it to America, Canada, throughout Europe and Scandinavia and as far as Australia. But it was the Royal flights that earned the Argonauts their greatest glory. One of the most memorable began on 31 January 1952, when Princess Elizabeth and the Duke of Edinburgh departed from London Airport for East Africa for the start of their Commonwealth tour. His Majesty King George VI was there to see them leave. Sadly, the King died a few days later, and the tour was cut short. Seven days after their departure, Queen Elizabeth II, clad in solemn black clothes that had been flown out to her, stepped wearily out of the same Argonaut and came down the steps, to set foot on British soil for the first time as Monarch.

The Argonaut's service record for BOAC was not, however without incident. There were two fatal accidents. The first occurred on 21 September 1955 as Argonaut G-ALHL approached Idris airport, Libya, in poor visibility, at night. The Captain attempted three landings, overshooting on each occasion. On the fourth attempt, the aircraft came in too low, struck a line of trees and crashed 1200 yards short of the runway threshold. Thirteen passengers and two crew members were killed. Less than a year later, Argonaut G-ALHE crashed on take-off at Kano, Nigeria, killing thirty two.

After a decade of service, BOAC retired the Argonaut on 8 April 1960, when Hotel Golf flew into London Airport from Abadan on the last service of the type for the Corporation. They had flown a total of 512,864 hours and carried 870,000 passengers.

The aircraft soon found a new lease of life with Overseas Aviation (Channel Islands) Ltd, a Gatwick based charter operator. This company used Hotel Golf and a number of other ex-BOAC Argonauts on inclusive tour flights to a large number of holiday destinations. Unfortunately, Overseas Aviation collapsed in August 1961 and the Argonauts were put up for sale by the controlling bank.

At this time Derby Airways (who would be renamed British Midland in 1964) were in desperate need of pressurised four-engined equipment. Lack of finance made the choice limited and they eventually decided to buy two Douglas DC-6A aircraft offered for sale by American Airlines. But with the collapse of Overseas Aviation, Derby Airways opted for the low priced Argonaut and purchased five aircraft. Two were cannibalised for spares at Burnaston Airport, Derby, and the remaining three entered service on inclusive tour flights, from Manchester, Birmingham, Bristol and Cardiff.

The choice of the Argonaut was, in the end, a bad one for British Midland. It was a decision they would come to regret primarily because of their high operating and maintenance costs. It soon became obvious that the Argonaut was tail heavy, and in a successful bid to improve longitudinal trim Hotel Golf was stripped inside. The rear lounge being replaced by relocated toilets, which solved the problem. At the same time an extra row of seats was added, increasing the capacity to seventy eight.

Because of airfield limitations, they could not be operated commercially from the grass runways at Burnaston, so the aircraft were based at Birmingham, where the airline leased hangar space, returning to Burnaston only for heavy maintenance and crew training. Despite landing and taking off empty the Argonauts badly rutted Burnaston's grass surface, and this could have been a contributory cause of an accident to Hotel Golf on 6 March 1967. The aircraft had just completed a local radio test flight, and upon touchdown suffered a nose wheel collapse. As a result, the aircraft was withdrawn from service for repairs. On completion, the aircraft was functionally flight tested by Captain Marlow on the 12 April, and found satisfactory. It was returned to service.

It was common knowledge amongst British Midland staff, that when Argonauts had been standing for long periods on the airfield, fuel was found to have transferred itself from one tank to another. This was mistakenly ascribed to mishandling of the fuel selectors by ground personnel. Pilots and engineers still believed that inadvertent fuel transfer in flight was an impossibility, even though a close examination of the fuel logs for Hotel Golf, and other Argonauts in the British Midland fleet, suggested that inadvertent fuel transfer in the air was a common occurrence, as the following incidents involving Hotel Golf will now show.

Hotel Golf at Manchester Airport in Derby Airways livery (Brian Robinson)

THE BEAUVAIS INCIDENT

On Saturday 13 May 1967, three weeks before the Stockport accident, Hotel Golf was found at Beauvais Airport, to be suffering a fuel leak in number 4 main fuel tank. The following day, the aircraft was ferried back empty to Castle Donington, under the command of Captain Hunt. On this flight number 4 engine was shut down and feathered. For fifteen minutes in every twenty to keep fuel distribution even while flying back on three engines, Captain Hunt fed engines 1, 2 and 3 from their respective main tanks, for the remaining five minutes he fed all three engines from number 4 tank. Captain Hunt noticed, that when number 4 tank was selected to off, and number 3 tank switched on, the fuel pressure rose not only on number 3 pressure gauge, but also on number 4. This should have been an indication that the tank selector lever for number 4 tank was improperly closed.

On landing at Castle Donington, Captain Hunt duly entered this abnormality in the technical log. Later a British Midland engineer checked Hotel Golf's fuel system, and found that no adjustment was necessary, and after a ground run, he entered in the technical log, under the 'action taken' column. 'Fuel cock checked and found satisfactory.'

Here as with other incidents, no diagnosis of the cause of the trouble had been arrived at.

Finally we come to the Palma incident, only one week before the Stockport disaster. What transpired on that flight was of such a striking nature, that if the facts had been reported and investigated, it would have led to the discovery of inadvertent fuel transfer. Even at that late stage, warnings could have been given to British Midland pilots operating Argonauts, to keep a careful watch on the outer main fuel tank states. If such a warning had been given, then Captain Marlow would have been in a better position to avoid, or at the very least, to cope with the emergency that was thrust upon him only one week later.

THE PALMA INCIDENT

On the morning of Sunday 28 May 1967, Argonaut Hotel Golf was in position at Ringway airport, ready to operate a charter flight to Palma, Majorca. The aircraft for this flight was under the command of Captain Barry Fleming, who occupied the left hand seat on the flight deck. To his right, acting as co-pilot sat First Officer Roger Wise, and behind them was Mr Gifford, an experienced, although not certificated, ground engineer. He was carried on the aircraft primarily to perform engineering duties during the periods the aircraft was on the ground at Manchester and Palma. He would also assist the Captain and First Officer during the flight with anything they might ask him to do, although this was not part of his official duties.

When Captain Fleming took over Hotel Golf from the previous crew, who had flown the aircraft into Manchester from Palma, a note left in the cockpit conveyed the information that number 4 fuel gauge was substantially under-reading, but no entry to that effect was entered in the technical log.

Hotel Golf had been refuelled with the standard load for the Palma run, namely, all four main tanks full and 100 gallons each in number 1 and 4 auxiliary tanks. With all cockpit checks completed, Captain Fleming taxied the fully laden airliner away from the stand, and turned the aircraft onto the runway. Lining up with the centre line, he advanced all throttles. Following a final check that all was in order, he released the brakes. Hotel Golf began to accelerate, and on reaching take off speed, Captain Fleming gently eased back on the control column and the aircraft became airborne at 10.07.

Climbing to cruising altitude, Captain Fleming levelled off and set a course on the first stage to Palma. At 11:10 using the fuel tank selector levers, Captain Fleming switched from main tanks to auxiliaries, and at 12.05, he switched back again to the main tanks. The engines were now being fed fuel from their own tanks, number 1 engine from number 1 tank, number 2 engine from number 2 tank, and so on. But unknown to the pilots, one or more levers controlling fuel flow was a few degrees out of position, and consequently, fuel in number 4 main tank was now being inadvertently transferred through a slightly open fuel cock to another tank.

At 14:50, when the aircraft was flying over the Perpignan region, the First Officer became concerned about the reading on number 4 main fuel gauge then showing only 350lbs. Even allowing for a substantial under-reading, with a consumption of about 460lbs per hour, this was cutting the fuel for number 4 engine rather close. There was nearly an hour to go before reaching Palma, and the possibility of having to hold there before landing. The First Officer asked Captain Fleming if he would like to cross feed from number 3 main fuel tank for a time, since this was showing a much higher reading. Captain Fleming replied that he had been informed that number 4 gauge was under reading, and that with full main tanks on take off, there must be enough fuel in number 4 tank to reach Palma with reserve. Consequently, he did not cross feed.

As Hotel Golf flew on towards Palma, the First Officer, still concerned about the number 4 fuel gauge low reading, asked the engineer to watch the fuel pressure gauge for number 4 engine, and let him know if it started to fall, so he could cross feed fuel from number 3 main tank to maintain a fuel supply to number 4 engine.

When Hotel Golf was approaching the runway threshold, something which the engineer did, was understood by the First Officer, to be a warning that fuel pressure in number 4 gauge was falling. He immediately moved the starboard cross feed selector lever to the midway inter engine position, to maintain the fuel supply to number 4 engine. He could not reach across to shut off number 4 main tank selector lever, without interfering with Captain Fleming's handling of the throttles on the final stages of the approach. The effect of cross feeding was to make the pressure indicated on the number 4 gauge to increase. Hotel Golf touched down almost immediately afterwards. At the end of the landing run, the First Officer told the Captain that he had opened the cross feed cock, which he then closed.

Captain Fleming taxied in on all four engines, so that Mr Wise could watch the pressures, which he found did not fluctuate.

Captain Fleming attached no importance to what his First Officer had told him about cross feeding, because he was utterly convinced that having started out from Manchester with full main tanks, sufficient for the flight, with reserve, there must be plenty left in all four main tanks on landing.

After shut down, the First Officer asked Mr Gifford to check the fuel uplift. This he did, noting down the quantities put into each tank to fill it to the brim on the refuelling receipt, as well as the total uplift, which is all he would normally have to record. The figures he got from the refuelling were in litres, and he and the First Officer worked out first the figures in gallons for number 4 main tank, which showed that it had only 14 gallons left on shutdown! After checking that the total uplift was correct, the First Officer came to the conclusion, that there must have been a mistake about the figures for the number 4 main tank uplift and rejected the result of the calculation as impossible. It did not occur to him to work out the uplift figures for the remaining three main tanks. If he had, he would have found that missing fuel from number 4 main tank had transferred itself into tank number 3.

The nature of the problem was never effectively communicated to Captain Fleming, or if it was, his reaction was the same as the First Officer, because of his conviction that full tanks on take off must mean plenty in hand, on landing at Palma.

On the return flight to Manchester, the First Officer kept a careful watch on the fuel system. He noticed no abnormalities, except for the substantial under reading he believed to be present on number 4 fuel contents gauge, and the fact that number 3 contents gauge became unserviceable during the flight.

The aircraft landed safely at Manchester, and later that evening returned to base at Castle Donington, landing there at 23:00. Mr Gifford, on Captain

Fleming's instructions entered as defects in the technical log, that number 3 fuel gauge was unserviceable, and that number 4 fuel gauge under-read by 400lbs.

The following day, British Midland engineers dealt with these defects, but not a word of what happened on the final approach to Palma, or the extraordinary result of the fuel uplift calculation reached British Midland's Chief Pilot, Captain Fenton.

Hotel Golf was now just one week away from disaster!

Chapter Six

SATURDAY NIGHT AND SUNDAY MORNING

Captain Harry Marlow was 41 and lived in the Nottingham suburb of Beeston. Like many airline pilots of his generation he first learnt to fly in the RAF, were he qualified in 1943 while serving as a non-commissioned officer. On leaving the service in 1954 he went on to obtain his Commercial Pilots Licence the following year. After serving six months with Skyways, a small independent charter company, he joined Derby Aviation, based at Burnaston aerodrome near Derby, as First Officer. The following year he was promoted to Junior Captain on Dakota and Marathon aircraft and in 1958 became Captain in Command.

Harry Marlow during his earlier flying days   (Bobbie Marlow)

At the time of the Stockport accident, he had amassed a total of 10,197 flying hours, of these, 2009 were on Argonauts. He held a current Air Transport Pilots Licence with Instrument Rating, and his licence was endorsed to command Argonaut, Viscount and Dakota aircraft. He had duly passed all his mandatory checks. In January 1967 he had an Instrument Approach Proficiency Check, his Instrument Rating was renewed in March and he passed his last medical in April. He also had line and route competence checks and was checked in asymmetric flying, including three engine take-offs and two engine landings. His base check on Argonauts included instrument approach, instrument overshoot, and approach and landing, all with number 4 engine shut down and with cross feed fuel drill.

From the foregoing, there can be no doubt that Captain Marlow was an experienced pilot and competent to command Argonaut Hotel Golf on flight BD542, from Palma to Manchester.

However, to give a true and accurate account of the story surrounding the Stockport disaster, mention should be made of a previous accident involving Captain Marlow. This occurred on the night of 14 October 1964, when he was in command of a British Midland Dakota - Juliet Victor - which took off from Hamburg, Germany, at 18:00 on a charter flight to Burnaston, Derby. With 36 passengers on board the main part of the flight was uneventful. After establishing radio contact with Derby air traffic control, Captain Marlow gave his estimated time of arrival as 21:00. The weather prevailing at Burnaston was passed to the aircraft, as surface wind calm, visibility two kilometres, no cloud.

Captain Marlow began a slow decent and the aircraft was cleared for an approach to runway 10. During the approach visibility began to deteriorate and the controller noticed shallow fog ahead of the aircraft. Captain Marlow, losing sight of the threshold lights, decided to overshoot at a height of 500 feet. He informed the controller that he would make another approach, this time to runway 28, and requested 'Very' lights to be fired from the runway threshold. Ground staff were dispatched with instructions to fire yellow 'Very' lights when the controller signalled with a green Aldis lamp from the control tower. However, before they were in position the Dakota had made its second approach and was in the process of overshooting when they arrived. Captain Marlow positioned the aircraft for a third approach, but this again resulted in overshoot action being taken at a height of 600 feet. Captain Marlow claims he did not remember making this approach, but according to the co-pilot, who did, the overshoot was carried out because the aircraft was not properly aligned with the runway, and he recalled seeing 'Very' lights to the left of the aircraft and a green Aldis light as the aircraft climbed away over the aerodrome.

Captain Marlow again positioned the Dakota for a fourth long visual approach to runway 28. The controller radioed the Captain that visibility was deteriorating and fog patches were on the aerodrome. Undeterred, Captain Marlow commenced his approach from approximately 4 miles out at a height of 1000 feet. He maintained visual reference by ground lights and by the lights of traffic on the A38.

When the aircraft was a mile and a half from the runway threshold at a height of 700 feet, Captain Marlow requested 'Very' lights because the runway lights were still not visible. Over Findern village, three quarters of a mile from the threshold at 500 feet, Captain Marlow saw the 'Very' lights and the first half of the runway lighting and was informed by the controller that the first gooseneck flares were now obscured by fog. A turn to the right was made to align the aircraft with the runway, and Juliet Victor with the undercarriage down and flaps extended swept across the runway threshold at 85 knots.

Drifting to the left, the aircraft touched down heavily on the port undercarriage, bounced, briefly became airborne and entered a bank of fog. Captain Marlow immediately lost visual reference with the runway and the Dakota struck the ground hard 70 yards further on collapsing the port undercarriage. The aircraft travelled across the aerodrome in a wide left hand turn, colliding with the perimeter fence and coming to a stop when the starboard wheel ran into a ditch.

At the runway threshold, the ground personnel who fired the 'Very' lights, saw the aircraft pass over with the engines throttled back and then disappear into the fog and presumed a landing was being made, but on hearing a thud drove back towards the control tower. The aerodrome fire tender also alerted by the noise drove down the runway, where visibility was between 30 and 100 yards. The aircraft could not be seen on the runway and was eventually located on the south-west boundary of the airfield. The aircraft was extensively damaged, but fortunately there was no fire and all the passengers and crew escaped from the aircraft without injury.

The findings of the accident report criticised Captain Marlow, in that, after three abandoned approaches, and the information given to him about the existence of fog patches on the aerodrome, it would have been prudent for him to divert.

British Midland was criticised for the approach lighting at Burnaston, which did not meet the required standard. Since they were responsible for the operation and upkeep of the aerodrome, they had a measure of direct control over the facilities provided for its aircraft operations. They were further criticised for allowing the aircraft to exceed the maximum authorised take-off weight. As a result of the accident, Captain Marlow was demoted to First Officer, but he was reinstated as Captain in June 1965.

The events culminating in the Stockport disaster began on Saturday 3 June. On that morning, Harry Marlow, taking advantage of his last day of leave, played a round of golf near his home in Nottingham. Later that evening he would return to duty at Manchester Airport to operate British Midland Argonaut G-ALHG - Hotel Golf - on a night charter flight to Palma and return.

His flight and cabin crew had left for Manchester earlier that morning by company transport from British Midland's base at Castle Donington. On arrival they took up rooms at the Excelsior Hotel near the airport where they spent the day resting - which was company policy - prior to taking up flying duties. Harry Marlow, preferring, as was his usual practice, to take his rest period at home, cancelled his hotel room the previous day through the operations room at Castle Donington, and at the same time arranged to collect some documents on the Saturday evening on his way to Manchester.

His game of golf over, he returned home, lunched, watched a sports programme on the television in the afternoon, then went to bed to read and sleep. At six pm he got up, showered, changed into uniform and set off on the 70 mile journey to Manchester Airport. On the way he called in at Castle Donington to collect the documents, only to find they had already been sent on. Continuing his journey, he arrived at Manchester Airport at nine pm. With an hour to go before the scheduled departure time, he went straight to the operations room where he met up with his flight crew.

Christopher Pollard who would act as his co-pilot, was 21 and came from Cornwall. He was remarkably gifted as a pilot having first learnt to fly at the age of 13 with the Plymouth Aero Club. At the age of 17, when he was legally allowed to fly solo, he gained his Private Pilots Licence. The following year he began training for his Commercial Licence and Instrument Rating at the London School of Flying, Elstree, where he graduated top of his group in 1965. He then joined British Midland Airways (who had sponsored him over the last part of his course) as Second Officer. To date he had flown a total of 1001 hours, 136 of these on Argonauts and his licence was endorsed to fly as co-pilot on Dakota and Viscount aircraft. Although only 21 years old, he was clearly an above average pilot with considerable promise.

Co-pilot Christopher Pollard   (John Pollard)

Gerald Lloyd, the third member of the crew, was 32 and lived in Kegworth. He was an experienced, although not a certificated, ground engineer. After service with the Fleet Air Arm he joined British Midland's predecessors, Derby Aviation in 1962 and served with them ever since. He flew as part of the crew in order to perform ground engineering duties when the aircraft was away from its home base. Nicknamed 'The Flying Spanners' these ground engineers had no duties to perform in the air, but in order to help out the crews during the flight they would fill in the instrument readings in the fuel and technical logs and operate switches and levers if asked to do so by the Captain.

In the operations room, Harry Marlow and Chris Pollard pored over their charts and studied the latest weather reports along the route. The forecast for the outbound flight was good with clear skies and light winds, but rain and overcast was predicted for the Manchester and Cheshire areas on their return. Completing the necessary paperwork they filed their flight plan to Palma and walked out across the tarmac to the waiting aircraft.

Hotel Golf, the Argonaut which Captain Marlow and his crew would take over, was involved in an incident at Manchester Airport the previous day. While taxiing out to the runway, a constant speed unit in one of the engines developed a fault. The aircraft aborted its take-off and returned to the departure gate where the passengers disembarked while the faulty part was replaced. After a two hour delay Hotel Golf took off, returning safely to Manchester on the Saturday morning where it stood on the tarmac all day awaiting the evening flight to Palma.

Before climbing the stairs to enter the cockpit, Captain Marlow walked around the aircraft, visually checking the control surfaces for any signs of damage, and the wings and engines for any leakage of fuel or oil. On inspecting the main landing gear he was not happy about the condition of one of the tyres and ordered it to be changed. While ground engineers jacked up the aircraft to change the wheel, Julia Partleton made the last minute preparations in the galley before the outgoing passengers boarded. Julia, an attractive 25 year old, experienced Stewardess, joined British Midland Airways in 1964. Rostered with Julia on this flight was Tony Taylor, from Leicester. Prior to joining the airline he worked in a hotel bar in London where one day he got into conversation with Julia's training stewardess. Bemoaning

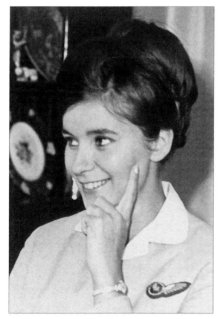

how dull the work was she suggested coming to work for British Midland as a Steward.

With the wheel changed, the Palma bound passengers boarded the aircraft. When the passengers were settled, Julia Partleton and Tony Taylor went through the safety drill ritual, pointing out the emergency exits and the location and use of the life jackets in the event of an emergency. Forward in the cockpit, Harry Marlow and Chris Pollard went through the start-up checks; a quick glance out of the side windows to make sure all was clear of the propellers and they were ready to

Stewardess Julia Partleton   (David Thorpe)

start the engines. The magneto switches were flicked on and the number 3 engine starter pushed. The three-bladed Hamilton Standard prop reluctantly turned a few silent revolutions and then the engine burst into life, sending a shudder through the airframe. The same sequence was followed for the remaining three engines and in a few minutes Hotel Golf was ready to depart the gate. The ground equipment was drawn clear. Harry Marlow glanced over his shoulder, checking the port wing was free of obstructions, Chris Pollard checked his side and called all clear, and with a 'thumbs-up' from the ground controller, Hotel Golf moved off the ramp with a burst of throttle.

The sun had long since slipped below the horizon as the Argonaut lumbered out across the broad expanse of the darkened airfield, picking its way between the sparkling taxiway lights. In the cabin, the passengers, with seat belts fastened were in buoyant mood, looking forward to their holiday in the sun.

On reaching the end of the taxiway Harry Marlow held the aircraft as he awaited clearance for take-off. The voice of the controller crackled in the pilots' headsets. "Hotel Golf, you are cleared for take-off." Harry Marlow acknowledged the message and steered the aircraft on to the runway. Lining up Hotel Golf's snub nose he reached for the throttles and pushed them gently forward. The noise of the four Merlins built up to a roaring crescendo, and when the RPM hit 3,000 he released the brakes. The Argonaut rumbled down the runway. Harry Marlow freed the nose wheel from the runway and the main wheels quickly followed, the rumbling ceased as Hotel Golf became airborne at six minutes past ten British Summer Time.

Immediately the aircraft left the runway Harry Marlow called for the landing gear to be raised, Chris Pollard complying, reached forward and operated the lever, the nose and main wheels responding, slowly retracted and clunked into their bays. The aircraft, now free of the excess drag from the undercarriage climbed away into the night, the lights of the airport gently slipping away beneath the tail.

Hotel Golf was soon crossing the south coast into the unrelieved blackness of the English Channel. In the dimly lit cockpit, the crew monitored the instruments and systems. The flight was seemingly routine and uneventful, but entries being made in the fuel log were showing abnormalities in the Argonaut's fuel flow and distribution. Yet again, as on previous flights, this went unnoticed by the crew.

Clearing the Channel, the aircraft crossed the coast and droned on over the darkened French countryside, relieved only by the clustered lights of the towns and villages that passed by far below. In the cabin the passengers dozed fitfully as the long hours passed, fatigued by the constant throbbing of the engines.

Five hours after take-off the shimmering lights of Palma floated into view over the nose, it was now nearing the time for the crew to begin the approach check. The disembodied voice of the Spanish controller broke the stream of static in the pilots' headsets with their landing instructions. The flaps were extended and the undercarriage groaned down. Three green lights on the control panel assured the pilots that the gear was safely down and locked. With landing lights on, Hotel Golf turned on to the approach and began to drop off height. The high intensity runway lights stretched out in front of the nose, like two rows of sparkling diamonds, drawing closer by the minute as the Argonaut nosed down through the wisps of cloud. As the Argonaut swept over the threshold, the throttles were pulled back to half power and the main wheels made contact with the runway with a screech. Time of touchdown was exactly twenty past three, British Summer Time. Breaking gently at the end of the landing run the Argonaut turned off the end of the runway and taxied to the terminal building.

Harry Marlow engaged the parking brakes and cut the power to the engines. After five hours of incessant engine noise and vibration the silence was overwhelming. Sliding off their headsets the pilots opened the cockpit side windows allowing the cold night air to penetrate the hot and stuffy flight deck. As the ground personnel manoeuvred the aircraft steps into position, Julia Partleton swung open the cabin door. The flight weary passengers shuffled down the aisle with their hand baggage, exchanging pleasantries with the stewardess as they disembarked. For them an enjoyable two weeks holiday lay ahead. For Julia, yet more more work, as she and Tony Taylor prepared the aircraft for the return flight. Harry Marlow and Chris Pollard left the aircraft for refreshments while Gerald Lloyd remained behind to supervise the refuelling. He uplifted the equivalent to that burnt off on the outward flight, which would be ample for the return journey with a reserve, if for some reason the aircraft had to divert. As in the Palma incident one week earlier, no calculation was made to ascertain the amount of fuel remaining in each of the four tanks after the flight. It is probable that the port and starboard outer tanks were almost dry on landing.

The early summer dawn had broken over Palma as the bleary-eyed returning passengers climbed the aircraft stairs, clutching bags of holiday souvenirs and presents. Harold Wood says, 'We had a wonderful holiday in Palma, good weather etc., who was to know what was to follow? We arrived at the airport in good time, and sat with some people we had met there. We were playing chess as the announcement for our flight was called. In those days it was one mad scramble to get the best seats. On the starboard side, were two seats together, then an aisle, then three seats together. My father went and sat at the front of the aircraft and my brother, Bill and I sat in the two seats on the starboard side, level with the wing. Behind us was a girl called Fiona and her friend Christine (Fiona Child and Christine Benton). Before departure we were told that we would be delayed because of an engine overhaul and we eventually took off at about five o'clock.'

One row from the front, on the starboard side, occupying the window seat was Vivienne Werrett. Next to her was her friend Susan Howarth. Vivienne says:

'We never went to bed that night. On the last evening of our holiday we went to an open air disco quite near the hotel. I remember watching one or two planes overhead and thinking that it wouldn't be too long before we were up there going home - worst luck!'

Behind them sat David Ralphs and Alan Johnson, from Staffordshire. In the same area was Mary Green and her holiday companion Linda Parry, both from Preston. All these passengers, because of their location, apart from Christine Benton, would survive. I have been unable to ascertain where Albert Owen sat, but it is probable that he too was seated in this area.

Harry Marlow and Chris Pollard, now back at the controls, began the engine start-up drill. One by one the four Merlins roared into life and very soon Hotel Golf was lumbering out towards the runway in the early morning light, as flight BD542 bound for Manchester. With the aircraft positioned at the end of the runway, the crew went through the 21 pre take-off checks. Holding the aircraft on brakes, the throttles were opened up, Harry Marlow momentarily paused as the needle hit 3000 RPM, assuring himself that all four snarling Merlins came up to scratch. Satisfied, he released the brakes and

Hotel Golf rolled forward steadily gathering speed eager to take to the air. As 110 knots was reached Hotel Golf heaved itself off the runway at six minutes past five British Summer Time.

With the compass needle happily set on a course for home, the flight was seemingly routine and uneventful. Unbeknown to the crew, a fuel selector lever was slightly out of position, and fuel was now slowly being transferred from the starboard outer number 4 tank down wing into the starboard inner number 3. Eventually number 4 tank would run dry, but number 4 engine would still continue to operate by drawing fuel back through the slightly open cock. This situation would continue until that lever was moved into the fully off position. When that happened number 4 engine would be starved of fuel and cease to deliver power.

Julia Partleton and Tony Taylor began serving breakfast to the sleepy passengers, most of whom were fitfully dozing, trying to catch up on missed sleep. Approaching Abbeville, France, at 08:36, Harry Marlow contacted London Airways who would route them over south east England and on towards Manchester.

Hotel Golf: *'London, Golf Alpha Lima Hotel Golf, good morning.'*

London: *'Hotel Golf, go ahead.'*

Hotel Golf: *'Hotel Golf, Abbeville three six, flight level six zero, Lydd five five, Rochester Brookmans Daventry Lichfield Manchester.'*

London: *'Hotel Golf, so cleared, maintain six zero.'*

Receiving clearance, the crew set a course that would intersect the Kent coast at Lydd. Twenty minutes later at 08:56, having cleared the Channel, Harry Marlow called up London Airways.

Hotel Golf: *'London, Hotel Golf, check Lydd at five six, flight level six zero, estimating Rochester at zero five.'*

London: *'Roger Hotel Golf.'*

Eight minutes later, at 09:04, Hotel Golf was approaching the outskirts of Rochester.

Hotel Golf: *'London, Hotel Golf, check Rochester at zero five, flight level six zero, estimating the Park at one five.'*

London: *'Thank you Hotel Golf, call Airways now on one two four decimal six. Good day.'*

Hotel Golf: *'One two four decimal six. Good day.'*

The Argonaut was now passed on to the next controller, who would guide the aircraft as far as Daventry. Harry Marlow dialled up the new frequency and called.

Hotel Golf: *'London, Golf Alpha Lima Hotel Golf.'*

London: *'Hotel Golf.'*

Hotel Golf: *'Good morning, check Rochester at zero five, flight level six zero and estimating the Park at one five.'*

London: *'Roger Hotel Golf.'*

Ten minutes later at 09:16 Harry Marlow called again.

Hotel Golf: *'London, Hotel Golf, check the Park at one six, flight level six zero and estimating Woburn at two six.'*

London: *'Roger Hotel Golf. What's your heading?'*

Hotel Golf: *'Hotel Golf, we're heading three one zero.'*

London: *'Roger Hotel Golf, turn right, heading three two five.'*

Hotel Golf: *'Right three two five.'*

At 09:26, Hotel Golf approached Woburn and called the controller.

Hotel Golf: *'London, Hotel Golf, check Woburn at two six, flight level six zero, estimating Daventry at three two, maintaining three one zero heading.'*

London: *'Roger Hotel Golf, resume your own navigation for Daventry, magnetic track is three zero five, over.'*

Hotel Golf: *'Hotel Golf, thank you.'*

Six minutes later, at 09:32, with Daventry passing abeam, Harry Marlow called London Airways for the last time.

Hotel Golf: *'Hotel Golf, passing Daventry.'*

London: *'Hotel Golf maintain six zero, call Preston on one two five decimal nine.'*

Hotel Golf: *'Roger, good morning.'*

Preston Airways would now control the last stage of the flight to Manchester. While Chris Pollard flew the aircraft Harry Marlow entered the new frequency on the radio and made contact with the Preston controller.

Hotel Golf: *'Preston, Hotel Golf, good morning. Daventry three two, flight level six zero, Lichfield at four five, Manchester. Over.'*

Preston: *'Roger Hotel Golf. Runway in use two four.'*

Hotel Golf: *'Thank you.'*

At 09:46, as Hotel Golf passed Lichfield, Harry Marlow, who had had little sleep during the last twenty four hours, began to make a number of errors in his radio transmissions with Preston Radar, and later with Manchester Control. Both pilots had been on duty nearly thirteen hours, then within the permitted maximum in force, and there can be no doubt that they were both suffering some degree of fatigue, Harry Marlow probably more so.

The problems of fatigue are particularly important to a pilot. Not only does he or she work long and irregular hours, but as distinct from almost any other job, theirs calls for peak performance at the very end of their period on duty, that of approach and landing.

Hotel Golf: *'Echo Golf, passed er... Lichfield five five, estimating Congleton at er ... , Sorry, four five, Congleton at five four, over.'*

Preston: *'Roger Hotel Golf.'*

Preston: *'Hotel Golf radar. The runway in use is two four, maintain flight level six zero to the Mike Charlie Romeo Beacon via Congleton.'*

Hotel Golf: *'Roger.'*

At 09:51, Preston Radar were dealing with a BEA Vanguard, Echo Delta, which also required routing into Manchester, and needed to descend through the Argonaut's flight level. Preston called up Hotel Golf to check their position.

Preston: *'Hotel Golf, what are your flight conditions?'*

Hotel Golf: *'I have Echo Delta in sight.'*

Preston: *'Roger, are you happy if he's to go through your level, he'll be number one at Manchester?'*

Hotel Golf: *'Affirmative, he's passed us.'*

Preston: *'Hotel Golf, continue with approach on one one niner decimal four. Good day.'*

Rain streaked across the cockpit windows as the Argonaut droned on through the drizzle-laden clouds towards Congleton Beacon. Chris Pollard continued to fly the aircraft as Harry Marlow changed the radio frequency in order to contact Manchester Approach, who would guide the aircraft down through the overcast on the Instrument Landing System (ILS) for a touchdown on runway 24.

Marlow: 9:56:00	*'Hotel Golf is just coming by Congleton, any instructions? Over.'*
Man.: 9:56:10	*'Roger Hotel Golf, you're re-cleared to flight level five zero and turn right heading zero three zero.'*
Marlow: 9:56:20	*'Right three three zero and we're steering three two five and released to five zero.'*
Man.: 9:56:30	*'Actually, zero three zero.'*
Marlow: 9:56:40	*'Right zero three zero and down to five zero.'*
Man.: 9:56:50	*'Correct.'*
Man.: 9:57:00	*'Hotel Golf, radar, continue descent to three five zero zero feet QNH, report passing five zero.'*
Marlow: 9:57:10	*'Roger, three five on one zero two zero, will check through five.'*
Man.: 9:57:15	*'One zero two five, Hotel Golf.'*
Marlow: 9:57:25	*'One zero two five ... Sorry!'*
Man,: 9:58:05	*'Hotel Golf, eight miles south east of the field, down wind left hand.'*

Flying at 200 knots Hotel Golf passed through the 4,000 feet mark in the descent. Harry Marlow and Chris Pollard started the approach check.

Man.: 9:59:35	*'Hotel Golf, turn left heading three five zero.'*
Man.: 10:00:25	*'Hotel Golf, turn left heading two nine zero.'*
Marlow: 10:00:35	*'Hotel Golf, Three five.'* (Harry Marlow reporting passing through 3,500 feet in the descent)

At this point in the approach check fifteen degrees of flap was extended and a slight increase in power was applied to compensate. All four engines continued to function normally, even though the number 4 starboard outer fuel tank was now completely empty. In the cabin the illuminated sign instructing the passengers to fasten their seat belts came on.

Man.: 10:01:27	*'Hotel Golf is nine miles from touchdown.'*
Man.: 10:01:35	*'Hotel Golf, seeing you well left of centre line are you receiving the ILS?'*
Marlow: 10:01:38	*'Yes, will turn right a little.'*

Chris Pollard banked the aircraft a few degrees to starboard to close with the ILS signal, and as part of the approach check reached forward, and with his left hand pushed against the fuel cross feed levers to make sure they were in the main tanks on, cross feeds off position. At that moment number 4 engine with its main tank already exhausted was being fed fuel through the slightly open cock from tank number 3. With the cross feed lever now properly closed, number 4 engine, now starved of fuel, ceased to deliver power at 10:01 and 55 seconds.

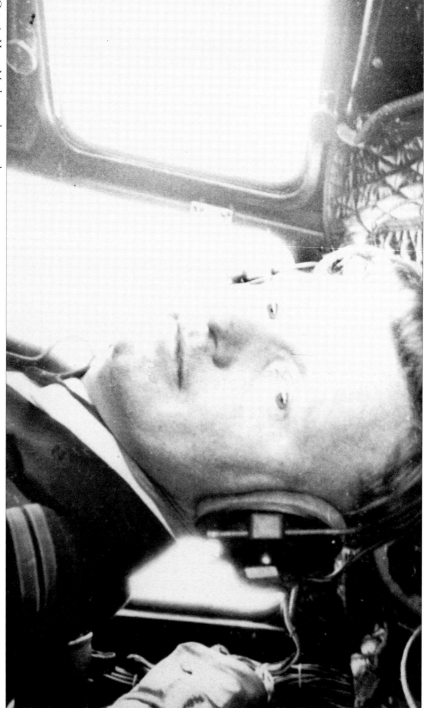

Chapter Seven

EMERGENCY OVER STOCKPORT

We will never know exactly what occurred on the flight deck when the number 4 starboard outer engine suddenly wound down. There were no cockpit voice recorders installed in civil aircraft in those days to tell us. But we do know that when Harry Marlow realised they had suffered an engine failure he immediately took over control of the aircraft from Chris Pollard. What happened next is matter of conjecture, but the following sequence of events fits in with the known facts.

Mistakenly believing that it was the number 3 starboard inner engine that had failed, and not number 4, Harry Marlow shut off its fuel, and ordered Chris Pollard to feather the engine. He then found that after cleaning up number 3 engine, it had not eased the handling problems associated with a single engine failure, and he was also losing height, which he should not have been with three engines under power.

At the height and position of Hotel Golf in relation to Manchester Airport at the time of the emergency it would have been possible for Harry Marlow to reach the runway and land safely, even with one engine feathered and the other windmilling. It is clear from the radio transmissions that he was perplexed by what was happening and took the deliberate decision to overshoot in order to try to sort it out, although in the end this decision proved disastrous.

Almost certainly number 4 engine failed first because of fuel starvation, its own tank empty due to inadvertent fuel transfer during the return flight, caused by an improperly closed fuel cock. If Harry Marlow did in fact misidentify the engine, it would have taken him some time to realise his mistake, if indeed he ever did. Once the correct identification had been made, there was in theory ample time available to sort out the mix-up, but with two engines out on the starboard side he was fully occupied in controlling the aircraft and trying to maintain height and heading. The remaining work load, navigation, communications and engineering greatly exceeded the capability of the First Officer, Chris Pollard.

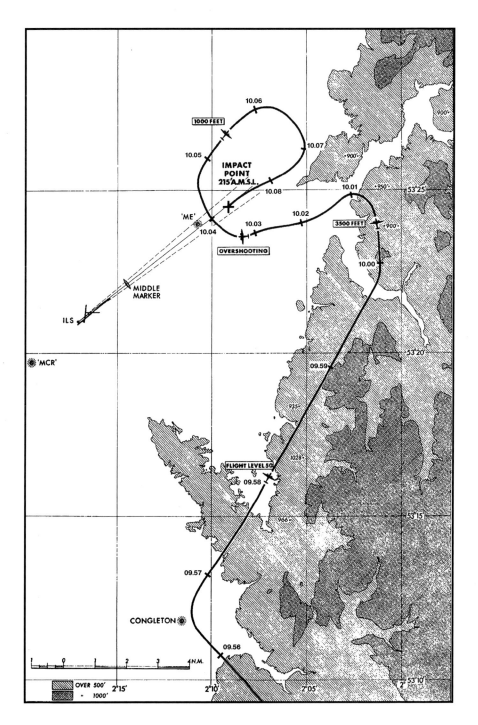

FLIGHT PATH OF HOTEL GOLF

90

At some point, after the mistake was realised, number 4 engine was feathered and number 3 unfeathered, but for some reason power was not restored to number 3 engine in time to prevent the crash.

What follows is the final seven minutes of Hotel Golf's flight, from the time the emergency occurred until the impact at Hopes Carr.

Man.: 10:03:07	'Hotel Golf is six miles from touchdown. Established?'

Hotel Golf did not acknowledge this message, seven seconds later the controller called again.

Man.: 10:03:14	'Hotel Golf radar do you read?'
Marlow: 10:03:17	'Hotel Golf is overshooting, we've got a little bit of trouble with RPM.'
Man.: 10:03:23	'Roger Hotel Golf.'
Man.: 10:03:30	'Hotel Golf make a left turn onto a heading one six zero climbing to two five zero zero feet on the QNH.'
Man.: 10:03:43	'Hotel Golf why are you overshooting?'
Marlow: 10:03:47	'We've got a little bit of trouble with RPM, ... will advise you.'
Marlow: 10:03:51	'What was the left turn onto?'

The controller saw on his screen that Hotel Golf had already turned through twenty five degrees to the right so ordered him to continue right and gave him a new heading. Hotel Golf's airspeed had now decayed to 114 knots and the altitude had dropped to 1,300 feet.

In the cabin, Julia Partleton, after stowing and securing equipment in the galley, slowly walked the length of the gangway from the rear, checking as she went that all the passengers had complied with the 'Fasten Your Seat Belts' instruction. Reaching the front bulkhead she entered the cockpit and gave the crew the 'thumbs up' that all was in order and they were ready for landing. She saw nothing untoward on the flight deck, the engineer was at his panel flicking switches and Captain Marlow appeared to her to be flying the aircraft. Nothing at all suggested to her that an emergency was taking place.

Closing the cockpit door behind her, Julia returned to the rear of the aircraft and strapped herself in next to Tony Taylor ready for the landing. As soon as she was settled in her seat the steward turned to her and said, 'I don't think we are going to get in.' Julia, thinking he was referring to the weather replied, 'Don't be so silly.' But on looking out of the window she thought to herself, we are a bit low. The steward turned to her again and said, 'He's taken the flaps back up.' Julia, who regarded Tony Taylor as a nervous type took no notice and sat back calmly awaiting touchdown.

Suddenly and unexpectedly Hotel Golf broke through the low overcast and from now on could be seen by witnesses on the ground. Beyond the rain streaked cockpit windshield, over the nose, a brick panorama loomed ahead. Harry Mallow glanced down at the altimeter and gasped at the frightful information it portrayed.

As the aircraft flew away from the airport in a wide right hand turn, it was seen by John Hamilton over Levenshulme flying north, all four props appeared to be turning and one engine was backfiring. By this time Hotel Golf's airspeed was down to 111 knots and was continuing to lose height.

Man.: 10:04:41	*'Hotel Golf advise when you're ready to recommence your approach.'*
Man.: 10:05:26	*'Hotel Golf your position is seven miles bearing zero four zero of the field. What is your level now?'*
Marlow: 10:05:32	*'ONE THOUSAND!'*
Man.: 10:05:35	*'UNDERSTAND ... ONE THOUSAND?'*

Pollard: 'AFFIRMATIVE.'
10:05:36

The controller was obviously staggered by this information, as this was the first indication that anything untoward was happening to the aircraft. After checking that the height given was correct he put full emergency procedure into operation at the airport.

Hotel Golf was now flying over the Gorton district where it was seen by off duty policeman Alan Faulkner.

'On that Sunday morning I had just returned from a friend's home. It had been raining and the cloud was low. The sound of a piston engine aircraft flying at low altitude attracted my attention and I looked up between the rows of houses. It was about 400 feet in altitude, certainly no more and I saw the large BM lettering on the tail and just below the tailplane on the fuselage were the words Canadair Four. The plane travelled in an arc towards the Audenshaw reservoir, flying with its nose up, tail down and a slight rocking of the wings.'

Man.:   'Hotel Golf can you maintain height?'
10:05:47

Marlow: 'Er ... Just about.'
10:05:49

Man.:   'Roger, you're eight miles from touchdown.'
10:05:51

Terrain clearance was now 625 feet.

Man.:   'Hotel Golf continue your right turn heading
10:06:18   two zero zero, maintain as much height as possible.'

The airspeed had now dropped to an alarming 98 knots, and the aircraft was in immediate danger of stalling and falling out of the sky. Harry Marlow in a desperate effort to keep Hotel Golf airborne pushed forward on the control column, forcing the nose down to gain more speed, in so doing sacrificing 341 feet of precious height in 15 seconds. The terrain clearance was now just 285 feet!

Marlow:	*'Hotel Golf; we're unable to maintain height at*
10:06:28	*the moment.'*

Man.:	*'Roger, you're eight miles from touchdown,*
10:06:33	*closing from the right.'*

Desmond Rea, a gas board official, heard the aircraft thunder over his home in Denton.

'I was in the house at the time and the engines seemed very loud. I came out into the back garden and saw the aircraft. There was nothing abnormal about it, apart from it being very low. I could make out the name on the side, British Midland, and the letters BM on the tailplane. The aircraft tried to gain height as it travelled towards Haughton Green, then it seemed to trail off behind the houses and dipped down very low.'

Man.:	*'Hotel Golf, I've lost contact with you, due to your height,*
10:07:09	*adjust your heading on the ILS and report established.'*

Pollard:	*'Hotel Golf, we have the lights to our right*
10:07:15	*and we are 800 feet this time, er ... just maintaining height.'*

(Chris Pollard mistook the lights in central Stockport for the airport approach lighting.)

Man.:	*'Roger Hotel Golf.'*
10:07:22	

Terrain clearance was now 290 feet.

Marlow:	*'Hotel Golf, will you get the emergency on?'*
10:07:25	

Man.:	*'Affirmative, the emergency has already been*
10:07:27	*laid on.'*

Marlow: 10:07:28	*'Ta.'*
Marlow: 10:07:35	*'Er ... what's the position from the field?'*
Man.: 10:07:36	*'Seven and a half miles to run to touchdown.'*
Marlow: 10:07:38	*'Thank you.'*

The next witness to see the aircraft was Ian McIntosh of Woodley to the east of Stockport.

'I saw the aircraft coming in from the direction of Hyde. It flew over a mill chimney in the river Tame valley north west from my home at about 150 feet. The nose was in climbing attitude and was flying very slowly. I had the impression it was really struggling to stay in the air.'

Man.: 10:08:12	*'Hotel Golf, I have no radar contact with you, you are cleared to land, surface wind two seven zero, twelve knots'*
Marlow: 10:08:17	*'Hotel Golf.'*
Man.: 10:08:25	*'Hotel Golf, I now have contact, six miles from touchdown.'*
Marlow: 10:08:28	*'HOW FAR?'*
Man.: 10:08:29	*'SIX ... MILES.'*

A Probation Officer saw the Argonaut's final moments of flight from Woodbank Park, where he was walking his dog.

'There was heavy drizzle and low cloud, I saw the airliner above the trees flying very low at about 150 feet. As the aircraft passed by I could make out the outlines of some of the passengers through the cabin windows. The aircraft then disappeared from my view and a few seconds later I heard the engines stop.'

Pollard: 'Hotel Golf, we're now 500 feet.'
10:08:32

Man.:   'Roger, your height should be 1850 feet.'
10:08:35

Pollard: 'Roger Hotel Golf.'
10:08:38

This was the last message received from the aircraft.

Hotel golf was now flying perilously low over the rooftops parallel to Turncroft Lane, heading towards the very centre of Stockport. Up to this point there was no sign of restlessness in any of the passengers, they were oblivious to the emergency taking place on the other side of the cockpit door.

Vivienne Werrett, looking out from her window seat, first became aware that something was wrong when she saw the gasometer pass by on the starboard side at the same level as the aircraft. She says:

'The roofs of the houses were suddenly becoming very close, we seemed to be opposite the bedroom windows. I looked out and I could see the street below, then the aircraft banked. I turned in my seat, grabbed hold of Susan's hand and said, OH MY GOD! and that was it.'

Harold Wood, seated a few rows behind says,

'I can remember as we were approaching Manchester a strong smell of perfume coming from the lady in front, which I thought was strange, as I hadn't noticed it during the flight. I reached up for the air conditioning, but it didn't seem to work. Looking towards the the front of the aircraft I could see that the 'NO SMOKING FASTEN SEAT BELTS' lights had come on.

'The aircraft then banked sharply to the right, and from the window, I could see a man walking out of a shop and getting into a Ford Anglia van, he then looked up at the aircraft. At this point I was feeling very nauseous and reached for the sick bag.'

Julia Partleton was still strapped in awaiting touchdown when a male passenger complained of feeling unwell. Unbuckling her seat belt she walked the short distance to the galley to fetch him a glass of water. Turning on the taps she suddenly heard a woman scream. Looking out of the window she was astonished to see the aircraft only a few feet above the rooftops.

The last seconds of the flight were now being being played out. In the cockpit the instrument dials became a confused blur as the Argonaut, now near to stalling, began to vibrate. Directly ahead, filling the cockpit windows was a row of four tower blocks barring their way. Hotel Golf had now reached aerodynamic exhaustion, and along with the crew gave up the unequal struggle to stay in the air. Cutting power to the remaining two engines, Harry Marlow banked the aircraft to the right over the roof of the Herbert Parks Tool Works aiming for a patch of green amidst a sea of buildings.

The airport controller, presuming the worst, continued to call the aircraft.

Man.: 'Hotel Golf, no radar contact.'
10:09:15

Man.: 'Hotel Golf, radar, do you read?'
10:09:30

Man.: 'Golf Alpha Lima Hotel Golf, do you read?'
10:09:45

The only reply was the crackle of static. There would be no reply... Hotel Golf had struck the ground at 10:09 and 5 seconds British Summer Time.

Chapter Eight

AIR CRASH DETECTIVES

Six hours after the crash, accident investigators from the Board of Trade arrived in Stockport, headed by senior inspector, Geoff Wilkinson. They immediately began work to discover the causes as to why Hotel Golf had crashed. Their investigation would prove to be long and arduous and one of considerable technical complexity.

After briefly examining the accident site they undertook the interviewing of eyewitnesses who saw the aircraft in difficulties at various points under the flight path, right up to the time of impact. However, their evidence, and that of the survivors gave the investigators no clues as to why Hotel Golf had suddenly within minutes lost speed and height over Stockport.

One vital witness, Captain Harry Marlow, who was pulled out of the wreckage alive, suffered retrograde amnesia in the crash, and could remember nothing of the flight beyond Congleton Beacon. He was interviewed by the investigators in Stockport Infirmary the following day. What he told them, allowing for the fact that he was still severely shocked and under sedation, was highly significant. He said, he couldn't hold the aircraft straight 'even with rudder' and had been trying to find somewhere to 'put the aircraft down,' but most telling of all was his question to the investigators, 'Which engine was it?' This and the evidence from his recorded conversation with the controller that he was having '... a little bit of trouble with RPM,' and the fact that Hotel Golf was rapidly losing speed and altitude, suggested to the investigators trouble with the engines or propellers.

Following this line of inquiry the engines were removed to the Scottish Aviation base at Prestwick, where Rolls Royce engineers stripped the four Merlin engines down to their 3,000 individual parts to determine if there had been any pre-crash malfunction or mechanical defect. Each component was cleaned, checked and, in some cases, x-rayed. The examination revealed that engines 1 and 2 on the port wing were operating at the time of impact, engine number 4, the starboard outer was stopped, and they made a new discovery about number 3 - it was probably windmilling - that is the propeller was being turned by the airflow and not by the engine. From all the available evidence there was no mechanical reason for the failure of these two engines.

The investigators now turned their attention to the propellers, which were examined by Hawker Siddeley Dynamics at Stevenage, to discover the blade pitch angles at impact. Because of damage sustained in the crash it was not possible to determine this from the damaged blades alone. They had to resort to impact markings made when the aircraft struck the ground. By this method they were able to conclude that number 4 propeller was feathered, and numbers 1, 2 and 3 were in the normal operating pitch. Again, as with the engines, there was no evidence of failure or malfunction.

At this stage in the investigation, all that was known with any certainty, was that Hotel Golf was flying with two of its four engines out of action for no obvious reason. Against this indisputable evidence, was the fact that none of the eyewitnesses who saw Hotel Golf during the last few minutes before the crash, speak of having seen any of the propellers stationary. There were nine such witnesses in all, and of those, four had served in the RAF and one in the Fleet Air Arm. In this instance their evidence about the propellers was regarded as unreliable, which is not surprising since they were all presented, some more suddenly than others, with the astonishing sight of a large four engine airliner, flying at very low altitude over a densely built-up area.

However, in the tail of the aircraft there was a reliable witness, the black box, in this case a bright orange armoured sphere. The Midas flight recorder was designed to survive the impact forces and fire of almost any crash, and if it was operating correctly the investigators could discover what had transpired during those last seven minutes of flight. The recorder was recovered undamaged and taken to the Royston Industries headquarters at Byfleet, Surrey. On examination the thin magnetic recording tape was found intact and had been running up to the time of impact. That tape could now be played back and would tell the investigators about the performance of the aircraft, the timing of every alteration in speed, altitude and heading, and at what point Harry Marlow lost the power of the two starboard engines. From the readout the Accident Investigation Working Group was able to reconstruct what happened during the last 900 seconds of flight.

This reconstruction conformed closely with the eyewitnesses evidence, and helped to fill the gap, which resulted from Harry Marlow's inability to remember anything about the final stages of the flight beyond Congleton beacon. It showed that number 4 engine failed first, followed twenty seconds later by number 3, just before the pilot radioed that he was overshooting. The airspeed then decayed to 110 knots and the behaviour of the aircraft was consistent with the pilot being faced with a major emergency involving severe control difficulties which were thereafter never overcome.

As factual information to help progress the inquiry this information added nothing, and gave no answer to the main question. Why were two of Hotel Golf's engines inoperative?

In September, three months after the accident, it was decided to carry out flight tests on Hotel Golf's sister aircraft, Hotel Yankee. The object of these tests was to establish the minimum control speeds with the aircraft in the same configuration as that of Hotel Golf in the last seven minutes of flight, that is with two engines out on the starboard side.

In good weather Hotel Yankee took-off from East Midlands Airport, Castle Donington. Flying the aircraft was Mr Davies, the Chief Test Pilot for the Air Registration Board and Captain Fenton of British Midland acting as co-pilot. Also carried as observers were members of the Accident Investigation Branch.

Mr Davies's general assessment of the controls was that the Argonaut was a rather heavy aircraft to fly, but that so long as all engines were operating there was no serious criticism to be made of its controls. However, with one or more engines inoperative its control characteristics were such, that though acceptable for transport aircraft when the Argonaut was offered for certification in 1949, it would not be accepted if offered for certification in 1967, because of the higher standards then set.

No passengers were carried on board Hotel Yankee, but enough sandbags were in place to simulate exactly the same load that had been carried by Hotel Golf on that last flight. On this test flight it was hoped to discover at exactly what speed the aircraft would stall carrying this weight, how it would behave at very low speeds with two engines stopped and whether it would have been possible for Captain Marlow to reach the airport.

The first thing they checked was the stall - the moment when the aircraft flies so slowly that the wings stop providing enough lift to keep the aircraft airborne. All four engines were throttled back, and as the airspeed dropped below 100 knots Hotel Yankee began to judder as the airflow broke away from the wings. With the aircraft in imminent danger of stalling and spinning out of the sky, they opened up the throttles, and with increased airspeed recovered and flew on. Next they shut down and feathered the number 4 starboard engine. This is how Hotel Golf would have been with only one engine stopped and the propeller as it was found after the crash. In this configuration Hotel Yankee found no difficulty in maintaining altitude, speed and heading. Now came the most potentially dangerous part of the test flight, with number 4 engine still feathered they shut down number 3 and allowed the propeller to windmill, meanwhile engines 1 and 2 on the port wing were operated at full throttle. In this situation Hotel Yankee's airspeed decayed rapidly, and to keep the aircraft on course the pilot had to use a great deal of physical strength in applying left rudder to counteract the asymmetric thrust of the port engines.

After a gruelling and hair raising two and a half hours in the air, Hotel Yankee landed safely at Castle Donington. For the investigators they had proved what they believed to be true but discovered nothing new and were no further forward. They still did not know why those two starboard engines failed when there was nothing mechanically wrong with them.

Within days of the disaster all the wreckage had been gathered together and transported by road to the Royal Aircraft Establishment at Farnborough for further examination. Lying in a vast hangar, like a giant jig-saw puzzle, all sections of Hotel Golf were reconstructed piece by piece - wings, fuselage, tail and engines. Little remained of the fuselage, just the burnt out shell around which the body panels used to be and the distorted metal framing of the seats. All the wreckage showed the signs of the horrific fire that ripped through the aircraft soon after impact.

If it was true that Harry Marlow had been having trouble keeping the aircraft straight, then the trim tab on the trailing edge of the rudder would be set well off centre. The trim tab was a small control surface designed to reduce the amount of physical pressure needed by the pilot on the rudder pedals. On inspecting the flight deck, the trim tab indicator was found set at 12 degrees nose left and confirmed the setting on the rudder as found after the crash. The reconstruction of Hotel Golf revealed no further clues and only confirmed what was already known.

In October, following a detailed analysis of the fuel logs of Hotel Golf and other Argonauts in the British Midland Fleet, it was decided to carry out ground tests on another Argonaut, Hotel Sierra - at Castle Donington. The object of these tests was to determine whether inadvertent fuel transfer might have had some bearing on why Hotel Golf's starboard engines failed when they did.

To test this theory they refuelled Hotel Sierra and started up the engines, then while still on the ground left the fuel cross feed lever - the lever that controlled the flow of fuel from different tanks to different engines - open by a fraction of an inch, a gap so small that neither of the pilots could see it when strapped in their seats. In this arrangement all four engines ran off their respective main tanks steadily using up fuel. After a period of time number 4 tank ran dry and the starboard number 4 engine wound down and

Argonaut Hotel Sierra

stopped. However, with engines 1, 2 and 3 running off their own tanks with the cross feed lever slightly open and with number 4 tank empty, it proved impossible to induce number 3 engine to fail either by fuel starvation or ingesting air from the empty number 4 fuel tank.

In light of these ground tests, the fuel logs were re-examined and revealed previous incidents of inadvertent fuel transfer in flight, which had not been diagnosed as such at the time, (see chapter five, The Palma Incident). The investigators had made a breakthrough. They could say with some certainty that if the cross feed lever was left just off the stops, then fuel could transfer from one tank to another. But this still did not explain why number 3 engine had failed.

Medical evidence disclosed that all the passengers who survived, with one exception, were seated at the forward end of the cabin on the starboard side. Their survival was fortuitous, because although they were in the area subjected to the maximum deceleration forces, they were in way of the large rent in the fuselage and so accessible to rescuers before the fire took hold. Of the 72 who died, 35 had died from burns, 15 from deceleration injuries and the remainder from head injuries and other causes.

It was never realised that the seats could be potential killers. The seats fitted in the Argonaut had two metal strengthening bars between the uprights, 9 inches above the floor. The bar nearest the passenger seated behind is comparatively thin, the inner bar was massive. Of the 66 seats examined, the thin outer bar was bent inwards or fractured in 38 cases, caused by the legs of passengers as the seats concertinaed forward in the crash. The consequent leg injuries sustained, resulted in the failure of conscious passengers escaping, or attempting to escape in what was a potentially survivable accident. It is difficult to imagine the horror experienced by those passengers trapped in the cabin, knowing that it was very likely to catch fire at any moment.

The Public Inquiry opened on the 28 November 1967, at 6 Burlington Gardens, a government building in London's west end, ironically not far from Regent Street and Piccadilly, where at the time most of the national and international airlines had their offices. The inquiry was conducted by Peter Bristow QC, with Captain Philip Brentnall and William Sturrock as assessors.

On the first day the public section of the inquiry room was crowded, and amongst the observers were relatives of some of those who lost their lives in the disaster. Evidence would be given from the accident investigators, representatives of the airline, Canadair the manufacturers and experts from every aspect of aviation. In all, sixty three witnesses would be heard.

Of all the people assembled on that first day, there was one person with more personal interest in the proceedings than anyone else - Captain Harry Marlow. During the following weeks he would sit listening to the background of that last flight. Every day the evidence was given, every known fact and relevant detail was brought out. Finally they came to the cross feed levers and how they affected the flow of fuel. Seizing on this information they adjourned the inquiry and ordered further tests to be made on the fuel system.

British Midland Argonaut, Hotel Yankee was flown to Boscombe Down where the fuel system underwent intensive testing. The engines were disconnected from the fuel system and replaced with pumps that would draw off the fuel at the rate used by the engines during flight. Fuel piping was replaced by clear tubing to see if air entered the system which might have been the cause of number 3 engine stopping. With this test rig it was hoped to discover not only how much fuel was being consumed by each engine, but if there was any cross feeding going on.

The results of these tests were of the highest significance. It was found that a slight misalignment of a cross feed lever could lead to fuel starvation of an outboard engine, but did not lead to any ill effects on the inboard engines, even with the cross feed cocks grossly open. During rig tests and engine ground running tests, no air was drawn into the system either before or after the outboard tank ran dry. The investigators, in the light of these tests, came to the conclusion that while it remained likely that Hotel Golf's number 4 engine ceased to deliver power as a result of fuel starvation, they still did not know why number 3 failed and the air theory had been totally disproved.

In March 1968 the inquiry was resumed and for another two weeks they puzzled over why the number 3 engine had failed.

When the inquiry was closed on the 1 April 1968, the assessors took

Harry and Bobbie Marlow with stewardess Julia Partleton at the public inquiry in London

(Stockport Express)

over, and for several months more, sifted and evaluated all the available evidence.

On the 22 August 1968, the inquiry published its findings. It reported:

'In our view there can be really no doubt that number 4 engine failed first, and failed because of fuel starvation from an empty number 4 tank due to inadvertent fuel transfer through an improperly open cock. We find it impossible on all the evidence before us to determine why the second engine failed. Following upon the Boscombe Down tests we considered the following possibilities.

'When number 4 engine failed it was misidentified as number 3, which was then feathered and its fuel shut off. Captain Marlow then found that the aircraft developed handling problems, and was losing height which it should not have been, and so came to the conclusion that the failure was in fact number 4. Number 3 engine was then unfeathered and number 4 feathered, but because of the high work load encountered by the crew, power was never restored to the number 3 engine in time to prevent the crash.

'The second possibility was that number 3 tank had also run dry because of inadvertent fuel transfer during the homeward flight, through fuel transferring across to the port tanks. When the cross feed lever was checked during the approach, fuel, until then feeding number 3 engine through the slightly open fuel cock from another tank, was cut off, number 3 engine would then fail almost immediately.

'To choose between these two possibilities would on the evidence before us be speculation.'

If in fact Harry Marlow did misidentify the engine it is not surprising, since the instrumentation in the Argonaut was crude compared with today's aircraft. Many of the flight instruments were dual pointer - that is, two pointers on the same dial - such as the RPM indicators. They are susceptible to being misread as the following incident shows.

On the 21 July 1950, a BOAC Argonaut was flying over the South Atlantic at 20,000 feet in darkness over smooth water. An engine which the pilot identified as number 4, overspeeded, he feathered the engine and almost immediately number 3 overspeeded and caught fire. The pilot managed to extinguish the fire at the second attempt, but could not feather the propeller. He was unable to maintain height on the remaining two port engines with the number 3 windmilling, so he decided to restart number 4, which he did successfully. Number 4 ran without trouble for some four hours until he made a successful landing at Fernando de Noronha.

Subsequent examination of the number 4 engine showed it to be serviceable and there were no signs of overspeeding. One of the conclusions of the investigation, was that the pilot may have misinterpreted the warning of the overspeeding due to the dual pointer and feathered number 4, when all along it was really number 3 that was overspeeding.

Fuel pressure gauges and flowmeters may well have aggravated the problem which faced Harry Marlow on the initial power failure, and his observation in the hospital on the day after the crash - 'Which engine was it?' - suggests they did, and must be regarded as being to a small extent a contributory cause of the accident.

Dealing with Captain Marlow's decision to overshoot, the inquiry said:

'Although in the event this decision proved to be disastrous, we think it was reasonable on his part to have come to his decision to overshoot, rather than carry straight on to an emergency landing, and for making that decision he was not to blame.'

The report went on to list the following contributory causes of the accident:

1. The failure of those responsible for the design of the fuel system or the fuel cocks to warn users that the failure to place the actuating levers in the proper positions would result in the risk of inadvertent fuel transfer.

2. The failure of British Midland air crews and engineers to recognise the possibility of inadvertent fuel transfer from the evidence available in previous incidents in flight and that in the fuel logs.

3. The failure of other Argonaut operators who had learned by experience of the possibility of inadvertent fuel transfer in flight and not informed the relevant bodies of those facts.

Because of the injuries he sustained in the accident Harry Marlow lost his licence. He said of the report:

'I am glad to know I have been cleared of blame. But I only wish I could get back to flying. Flying has been my life since I joined the RAF during the war, and I still think I could fly again. I think they have given me a certain amount of praise for getting the aircraft down in this particular place. If there had not been that fire there certainly would have been a lot more people saved from the aircraft. I agree with the report, I rather anticipated this would be the result of the inquiry. That fuel trouble … there was no way of anyone knowing.'

Chapter Nine

THIRTY YEARS ON

THE CRASH SITE

Walk down Waterloo Road and into Hopes Carr today, and you will find little sign of the events that occurred there thirty years ago. The Hopes Carr sub-station which was partly demolished when the starboard wing ploughed into the back wall was rebuilt shortly afterwards and still stands, and if you know where to look you can faintly see where the new brickwork interlocks the old. The garage forecourt area surrounding the sub-station where the fuselage came to rest, is now a 'pay and display' car park. Yates's garage opposite, where the first bodies were taken, has since been extended. On the corner of Waterloo Road, the row of terraced buildings, hit by the port wing as the Argonaut came down, lay derelict and boarded up for sometime, eventually being demolished in 1969. The grassy slope leading down to the stream, where Hotel Golf's fire blackened tail section lay wrecked, has been reclaimed over the intervening years by trees and dense undergrowth, hiding all signs that a disaster ever occurred there.

HARRY MARLOW Captain

Harry Marlow joined the RAF during the Second World War, and like many other would-be pilots, was sent to Canada for basic training, gaining his wings there in 1943. Returning to the UK he was posted to RAF Church Fenton where he lived in married quarters with his wife, Bobbie. During his time there he converted to fly the new Gloster Meteor jet fighter, eventually becoming a member of the aerobatic team.

Leaving the RAF in 1954 he obtained his Commercial Pilots' Licence and joined Skyways of London, flying Avro Yorks and Hermes transport aircraft. In January 1956 he took up the post of First Officer with Derby Aviation and served with them up the time of the Stockport accident.

Because of the injuries he sustained in the crash he was deemed medically unfit for flying duties and his licence was withdrawn. Swapping airliners for

A recent photo of Harry Marlow   (Bobbie Marlow)

washing machines, he invested his savings in a coin operated laundry, in Borrowash, Derbyshire in 1969. At the time he said:

'I am determined to get back in the air. I will give it a bit of time and then go for another medical.'

Sadly, Harry Marlow never flew again. Now in his seventies he lives quietly in retirement in Chilwell, Nottingham, and still plays the odd game of golf.

Since the disaster he has never given interviews, and on the one occasion I spoke to him he refused to discuss the accident. In a letter Mrs Marlow wrote to me a few weeks before the memorial unveiling, she said of her husband,

'Flying was his life, and all that came to an end on the 4 June 1967. We will always have to live with that.'

CHRISTOPHER POLLARD Co-pilot

Christopher Pollard was born on 6 April 1946 in Plymouth, the second son of Hartley and Ann Pollard. The family moved to Marazion, Cornwall, where Chris started school travelling daily into Penzance, but finished his primary education in Plymouth, having returned to that city in 1955. He went on to finish his schooling at Queen's College, Taunton and Plymouth Technical College. In 1964 he entered the London School of Flying before joining British Midland in September the following year. He lived at The Plough Inn, Diseworth, close to Castle Donington airport, although he frequently returned to Cornwall where his parents had retired in 1965.

His interest in flying developed very early. What prompted it is difficult to say, there being little flying activity in Cornwall to stimulate the imagination, apart from the annual airshow at Culdrose, which the family often attended. An occasional trip to London would involve the whole day

Co-Pilot Christopher Pollard   (John Pollard)

at the observation centre at Heathrow. He was good with his hands, and started modelling Airfix Kits, before moving on to build powered balsa wood models, whose engines he would spend many an hour patiently trying to coax into life before flying them up on Dartmoor or, in his free time at school, in the vicinity of Taunton. He read as many books as he could about flying, and was particularly stimulated by Philip Cleif's 'Airway to the Isles' which concerned the route to the Scilly Isles, west of Lands End. Cleif was based at Roborough in the early 1960s and was one of those that taught Chris to fly. By the time he was in his mid-teens he lived and breathed flying. As soon as he was able, he took flying lessons on Tiger Moths and Austers at Plymouth's Roborough airport, and got his private pilot's licence as soon as he was legally able to fly solo.

He had many other interests, including amateur dramatics and sport, but, from a career point of view, he was not interested in anything desk-bound or too academically based. Nothing but a life with the airlines really appealed, and so he applied to the London School of Flying at Elstree. He progressed well there and, although his studies were first financed by his father, British Midland sponsored him over the last part of the course. He was quick to learn and sailed through his practical and theoretical tests without difficulty. There is a report that he passed out at the top of his group at Elstree but, being a modest chap, he never made anything of this. His time at Elstree and subsequently at Castle Donington with British Midland was the happiest time of his life. He had not taken easily to boarding school life in Taunton, although he did come to terms with it in the end, but now he was in that enviable position of his hobby being his job. He was a kind, considerate, outgoing individual, who quickly made friends. He had settled in well with his colleagues at Castle Donington, and was technically very capable. He quickly qualified to fly both Viscount and Argonaut aircraft. He had also recently become engaged to Helen Jones, who then worked as a stewardess with British United, and so all was perfect in his personal life too. Tragically it all came to an abrupt end.

Julia Partleton after her return to flying with Air International (David Thorpe)

JULIA PARTLETON Stewardess

Julia was born in Ruskin College, Oxford in 1942, her mother having been evacuated from Stockwell in London during the blitz. Sadly her mother died of TB in 1946 and she was then brought up by her grandmother, until she too died, leaving Julia to fend for herself from an early age. Although she seldom spoke of this part of her life, it undoubtedly had a considerable affect on her, making her very proud and very determined, underneath which was a very caring person, champion of the underdog, and passionately fond of animals.

She was educated at Stormont House School in London. Her first job was as a

Julia Partleton   (David Thorpe)

secretary at St George's Hospital, London, where she stayed until 1964, when she left to join Derby Airways at Burnaston, Derby, as a stewardess. Although the records show that she worked hard and had various commendations as a stewardess, she clearly 'worked hard and played hard', and undoubtedly this was the happiest time of her life.

Following the Stockport accident, from which she suffered a broken back and first degree burns to thirty five percent of her body, followed by months of plastic surgery to her legs, she eventually went back to flying. Indeed, the day she left hospital, she went straight to the airport and flew as a passenger to Palma!

Once fully recovered - if one ever recovers from the trauma of such a horrific accident - she resumed flying duties with British Midland and later went on to fly with Air International. After leaving flying, she worked at the Brook Street Bureau and United Biscuits. She also had an interest in a furniture business in Ilkeston, Derbyshire, with her partner of many years, David Thorpe. At the same time she restored an old cottage in Castle Donington, actually putting in the damp courses herself. This became her cherished home for many years, which she shared with her friend Sam, a German Shepherd, and three stray cats.

Julia travelled widely with David, visiting such places as New York, New Orleans, Rome, Naples and Spain. David said, 'Julia was usually tense during take-off and landing but otherwise had no difficulty in flying.'

Ironically Julia died on Sunday 20 October 1996 in the Derby Royal Infirmary. The following day my request seeking her whereabouts appeared in the Derby Telegraph.

David said: 'It will always remain a question of debate as to how Julia would have reacted 30 years on to the remembrance services and general publicity, as she rarely spoke of the accident. Having said that, she left a very comprehensive scrap book of all the press cuttings of the day, as well as saving the letters and cards from all the flowers she received, but again, she never showed them to anyone.

'My own feelings, when attending the memorial service in June 1997, was still being very upset about her untimely death, I nevertheless felt some gratitude for the 'extra thirty years' which Julia had, had she not unfastened her seat belt and walked down the cabin to fetch a passenger a glass of water.

'Her death occurred some two years after suffering a severe stroke to the right hand side of her body, which seriously affected her speech. As a very proud and independent lady, this came as a devastating blow to her. I well remember the day she came out of hospital - where she had spent four months - and came face to face with the aids which had been made ready, pending her return home. She took one look at a commode which had been installed downstairs, whereupon she literally forced herself upstairs despite the fact she had the use of only one arm and one leg. I recall another incident which demonstrates her independence - I found her trying to get ready to go out, and when I asked her where she was going, the answer was that she had to try and get back to work! Many people, in similar circumstances, would probably have been thinking about allowances, insurance claims etc - to Julia, these were all offensive words as they denoted dependence on others, or even failure.

'During the two years of the stroke, together with her good friends Sylvia, Jean and Derek, Jill and Conroy, and her carer, Sue Mooney, we all ensured that she lived as full a life as possible. I remember taking her Christmas shopping in Derby - she loved Christmas - and she was so eager to make sure that she had a present for everybody, especially the cats. We all helped with the wrapping up. I remember wondering how many of us would have been so keen to buy presents for everyone, whilst suffering so many afflictions ourselves.

'It was in the last three months leading up to her death that she began to plateau in her recovery process, eventually becoming breathless with increasing frequency. The doctor said she was hyperventilating, and advised that she breathe into a paper bag. When the breathlessness clearly was becoming unacceptable, she was admitted to the Derby Royal Infirmary, where she was diagnosed as having possible pneumonia, and transferred to a chest ward. In the month which followed she seemed to deteriorate, and indeed she relied totally on her oxygen mask. Two days before she died, it was eventually established that she had a myxoma on her heart, which by the time it was discovered, was a massive 5 x 7 centimetres. This was not malignant, and although its removal would have involved open heart surgery, it would have been a very survivable operation. Sadly she died the day before its planned removal.

'I asked for an Independent Review of the situation, which has since confirmed that there were sufficient early warning signs for the specialists to have taken earlier action. It seems very sad that such a kind and caring person should have died through the carelessness of others, particularly as she survived two serious car accidents - one in which a lorry crossed the central reservation on the M1 - and of course Stockport.'

Julia is buried in Castle Donington cemetery, which ironically backs onto the perimeter of the East Midlands Airport - it was from here that she flew so often, during what must have been the happiest years of her life.

VIVIENNE WERRETT Survivor

When Vivienne Werrett (now Thornber) regained consciousness after the crash, she found herself trapped and her left leg badly smashed. With flames coming towards her she screamed. It was those screams that alerted PC Bill Oliver who hauled Vivienne and her friend Susan clear, minutes before the aircraft exploded.

Thirty years later, Vivienne and her husband Chris celebrated their silver wedding. She says:

'I still get nightmares from time to time, although physically I have recovered remarkably well. The doctors thought I would lose my leg but they saved it and I don't even have a limp. It was inconceivable thirty years ago, looking at the state of my completely shattered left leg that I would walk again, let alone live life at the pace I do now, looking after my home, working full time and having my musical hobbies.

'I am living a very full and active life, being a member of three local operatic and dramatic societies. In 1997 I successfully auditioned for the female lead in 'The King and I', but the most taxing thing to date was playing the 'Julie Walters' role of Vera in 'Stepping Out'. I really didn't know when offered the part how my legs would stand up to the demanding tap dancing routines involved. It was a personal triumph for me, not only when I achieved it, but was nominated for an award for the part. None of that seemed remotely possible thirty one years ago.

'What happened has made me live each day at a time rather than looking too much to the future, and I value every minute. I didn't realise how precious life is.'

Two years after the disaster Vivienne and Susan returned to Majorca, and she has flown regularly every year since.

'I still fly because I love travel and the sun. I cope fairly well, but I do prefer to sit in the same seats as on the Argonaut on that fateful day. It feels strangely comforting knowing they were lucky for me then. Unaccountably, it is the take-off which is my worst moment. I am reasonably calm on landing which seems strange given the circumstances of the accident.

'I must admit to being moved by the sight of the Salvation Army band at the recent memorial unveiling and service, particularly when they played 'The Lord is My Shepherd'. Memories were suddenly very clear of the Sunday following the accident when the band came into the infirmary and played that same hymn which has come to mean so much to me.'

Vivienne's friend, Susan Howarth died suddenly in February 1998.

DAVID RALPHS Survivor

David Ralphs suffered third degree burns in the accident and was hospitalised for three months. He then endured a series of skin graft operations over a three year period. For many years he was reluctant to fly, preferring to take his holidays by car or coach, but in recent years he has taken to the air again and plans to fly to Canada next year.

He now lives in Newcastle-under-Lyme with his wife, Rosalie, and is Managing Director of a company manufacturing industrial textiles and work wear. He has two daughters, Debbie and Helen.

His friend, Alan Johnson who also survived, died in 1995.

HAROLD WOOD Survivor

Harold Wood who walked out of the wreckage with minor injuries, says, 'I was one of the lucky ones. Apart from partial deafness in my right ear I only suffered cuts and scratches. Since that experience I have flown all over the world. Today I am married to Linda and have two children, Matthew, aged 19 and Christina, aged 17. We have been running 'The Cross Swords', a country inn and restaurant in Skillington, Grantham, for the past seven years.

'Looking back I think a lot more people would have been killed if it hadn't been for the skill of Captain Marlow putting the aircraft down when and where he did.'

Harold's brother Bill now lives in Kettering.

Survivors Vivienne Thomber and David Ralphs at Stockport Town Hall on the 30th Anniversary

(V. Thomber)

120

Of the other survivors, Mary Green is still alive and living in Preston. When I made contact with her she declined to be interviewed and wished to take no part in either the book or the 30th anniversary memorial service. Her close friend and holiday companion, Linda Parry who also survived, died some years ago.

Fiona Child, the only survivor from Stockport, was shielded from all publicity at the time. I have tried to make contact with Fiona via her parents without success and can only conclude that this is a part of her life she wishes to put behind her.

Albert Owen, from Eastham in the Wirral, who staggered out of the wreckage to be met by Bill Oliver, lost his wife Eva in the accident. I have unfortunately been unable to trace him. If he is still alive he will be now in his late eighties.

PC Bill Oliver, the first police officer at the scene, died in 1976 of a heart attack at the age of 42. He was undoubtedly one of the heroes of the disaster and many of the survivors owe their lives to him because of his prompt actions that day.

Born in Hazel Grove, Bill attended Mile End School and his first job on leaving was as a clerk with British Railways.

PC Bill Oliver being presented to Prince Philip (Ruth Oliver)

When called up for National Service, he joined The Royal Military Police and was a member of the International Police Force in Vienna. After National Service he joined the British Railway Police in Manchester before moving on to the Stockport Borough Police Force as a constable in the mid 1950s. He was on beat patrol until 1964 when he became one of the first policemen in Stockport to take up motorcycle patrol duties. His widow, Ruth, now lives in Anglesey, North Wales.

Pauline O'Sullivan, who lost her parents, brother and cousin in the disaster, always wanted to make a pilgrimage to Majorca, but for years refused to travel by air. But in October 1995, she made the journey with her husband Ted. Pauline said:

'Mum sent us two postcards while on holiday in Majorca and I always wanted to go there some day to visit the places they visited and find the hotel where they stayed. But the main reason I didn't go before was that I had been afraid of flying since the air crash. My husband Ted always reassured me how safe it was, as he had flown all over the world when he was in export sales. I must admit every time we said goodbye before those trips I wondered if he would come home safe - remembering that day in May 1967 when I said my last goodbye to mum, dad, David and Philip. Eventually, I realised I would never be able to visit Majorca if I did not overcome my fear of flying. Although I do fly now, I always shed a tear of relief when we land, especially at Manchester.

'While in Majorca we stayed at Puerto Pollensa in the north of the island, and hired a car to visit the places mentioned in the postcards mum had sent us. Valldemosa was one, a beautiful village in the mountains where Chopin

Hotel Bon Estar, Majorca   (Pauline O'Sullivan)

stayed in 1838. One evening we went on an organised trip to an old Mallorcan Palace, possibly the same one the family visited to see a display of Spanish folk dancing.

'One of the postcards from mum and dad had a picture on the front of Cala Mayor, Palma, which is where our search for the Hotel Bon Estar was concentrated. We asked hoteliers, bar owners, the tourist information centre and even the Federation of Hotels, but no one had heard of it. I knew that after so many years it could have changed its name or may be no longer a hotel. Even so, I was really disappointed.

'However, on our flight back I was sitting next to a lady (Deirdre 'Dee' Wade) and got chatting. She had lived in Majorca for seven years with her husband and family and was returning home to the Lake District for a holiday. I told her about our unsuccessful search for the hotel Bon Estar and she promised to try and find out where it was when she returned to the island.

'Several months later, to my surprise and delight a bulky letter arrived from Dee Wade. After a series of appeals in the Majorca Daily Bulletin, the hotel had been located in Ciudad Jardin, which was to the east of Palma. It was in the first stages of demolition.

'Dee and I have kept in touch ever since, and I know she will be interested in the memorial to the victims of the air crash.'

The hotel was the last link in the tragedy, and now it has been found, Pauline feels she has completed a cycle. In doing so, she has also discovered a beautiful island and acquired some happier memories.

For British Midland it was the company's worst ever disaster and for the Argonaut the writing was on the wall. Their history had not been a happy one. During their time with the airline they suffered a long series of in-flight engine failures causing delays and diversions, so much so that one large tour operator transferred all its business to the rival airline Cambrian. The two remaining Argonauts did not fly on public transport service again after the 1967 season. Hotel Sierra was withdrawn from service on 16 October, and Hotel Yankee on 6 November 1967. Both were sold to Chartwell Aviation on 19 October 1968 and later scrapped.

Brian Donohoe, one of the first civilian rescuers on the scene still has a baker's shop on Hillgate. The only recognition he received for his efforts was

Brian Donohoe recalls events for GMR Radio (Steve Morrin)

a watch from Fiona's parents, bearing the inscription, 'Thank you for saving Fiona's life.' This watch has since been snatched by thieves in a break in.

As the 30th anniversary of the disaster approached in 1997, there was a great deal of interest in the town, and both Brian Donohoe and myself were in demand for interviews from the press, radio and TV. It was after one such interview that Brian and I decided that this anniversary should not go by without some sort of memorial service.

On Sunday 8 June, survivors, rescuers, ex-members of the police, fire and ambulance services, along with members of the Salvation Army, gathered on the corner of Waterloo Road and Hopes Carr. At 10:09, the exact time that Hotel Golf crashed, the Reverend Arthur Connop MBE, commenced a short memorial service for all those who lost their lives at this spot thirty years ago. A wreath of seventy two red carnations was laid at the site by survivor Vivienne Thornber. She also laid a single red rose in memory of her rescuer, PC Bill Oliver.

A week or so after the service, Bertha Thorniley said to me. 'The thing I appreciate about all this was being there at the memorial service and seeing two survivors and being able to talk to them. Because those are the two people I will hang on to and remember. Arthur and I have talked about this, and that was the best thing that has happened for us - being able to talk to two people who survived, instead of having the memory all the time of the people who didn't.'

Survivors and rescuers at the 30th Anniversary memorial service
at the crash scene - June 1997   (Lynn Talbot)

Brian Donohoe and the author

(Manchester Evening News)

SEVENTY TWO
IN MEMORY
OF THE
AND PASSEN
WHO LOST CREW
STOCK
IN THEI

Chapter Ten

IN MEMORIAM

At the time of the 30th anniversary, many questions were asked as to why this spot had lain unmarked all these years. This was a question I couldn't answer. I did know from my research that plans had been drawn up and money allocated for a memorial garden on the site in 1977 for the 10th anniversary, but for various reasons these proposals were never carried through. Considering this was Stockport's greatest catastrophe and one of the worst civil aviation accidents at the time, it was, to to my mind the 'forgotten disaster.' It was then that I made the promise that a permanent memorial would be in place before the next anniversary.

To this end Brian Donohoe and I enlisted the support of Stockport MPs Ann Coffey and Andrew Stunell, who made the first moves on our behalf. There then followed a number of meetings with the local authority where we outlined our proposals, which, I am pleased to say, were readily accepted without reservation.

From the beginning of 1998 I put the writing of this book aside and all my efforts went into tracing the relatives of those killed so they could have the opportunity to attend the memorial unveiling, which was set to take place on the first Sunday in June. With a time span of thirty one years, this proved to be a difficult task, but within six months I had managed to trace the majority of them, some as far away as Canada and Spain.

IN MEMORY
OF THE
SEVENTY TWO PASSENGERS
AND CREW
WHO LOST THEIR LIVES
IN THE
STOCKPORT AIR DISASTER
4th JUNE 1967

Receiving tremendous support from them all, plans were then drawn up for the memorial in its final form. The choice of the stone I left

Stonemason Bill Stevenson installing the memorial (Author)

in the hands of stonemason Bill Stevenson of Granart Memorials, Chapel-en-le-Frith, Derbyshire. I was not to be disappointed, the end result was superb.

The week leading up to the memorial unveiling and remembrance service was a period of frenetic activity. As we put the final arrangements into place, the media descended upon us, with the press, radio and television all clamouring for interviews. One interview with Radio Five Live was broadcast nationwide - the 'Forgotten Disaster' was forgotten no more.

Relatives, rescuers and survivors gather on the corner of Hopes Carr

The Reverend Arthur Connop MBE conducts the memorial service

Reverend Arthur Connop MBE

The day of the memorial unveiling and remembrance service, Sunday 7 June, dawned with little promise - rain and overcast skies - weather almost identical to that tragic Sunday morning in 1967. With umbrella in hand, I was at the memorial site early to greet all those relatives I had corresponded with over the last few months. Today we would meet face to face for the first time.

The morning began appropriately with the Salvation Army Band - who gave so much help at the time of the disaster - marching from the Hillgate Citadel into Waterloo Road. After a short address by the Mayor of Stockport, Councillor Gordon Cooper, the service got under way, with the Reverend Arthur Connop MBE officiating. I especially asked Arthur to conduct the service, as at the time of the disaster he was Chaplain to the Stockport Borough Police, Fire Service, Ambulance Service and Stockport Infirmary, and was known personally to many of the relatives and others attending.

Despite a heavy downpour of rain, the Service was an extremely emotional and moving occasion, with Vivienne Thornber, accompanied by

Bob Greaves with survivor Harold Wood

Survivor Vivienne Thornber unveils the Memorial

fellow survivors, David Ralphs and Harold Wood unveiling the memorial. A Civic Reception was held afterwards at Stockport Town Hall, giving those attending the opportunity to renew old friendships and, in some cases, form new ones.

The memorial stands, not only as a fitting tribute to those who died, but also to the many silent and unknown heroes of Stockport, who risked their lives that day in the desperate effort to save the passengers of Argonaut Hotel Golf.

I consider myself very privileged to have been accepted into this special group of people, united by those events which happened thirty one years ago. I hope I have - to use the words of Arthur Connop - aided them to come out of the shadow of their grief and associate with others, making a transition, from a 'Fellowship of Suffering' to an alliance of 'Thankful Remembrance.'

THE END

BRITISH MIDLAND AIRWAYS

The origins of British Midland Airways stretch back sixty years to 1938, when the company began flying as Air Schools Ltd, specialising in pilot training. On the 29 September of that year they began operations at Burnaston Aerodrome, Derby. This consisted of a grass runway and a single Bellman hangar. A rundown stately home was put to use as an Officers' Mess and club house. When war broke out the Air Ministry asked Air Schools to run a second school at Pendesford, Wolverhampton. With both schools running at full strength they trained a record 14,000 pilots, set the best maintenance record and the lowest accident rate.

With the ending of hostilities in 1945 the Air Ministry contracts were terminated. As a result, the company diversified its operations and began ad hoc passenger and cargo charter work with a fleet of light aircraft and some eight-seat de Havilland Dragon Rapides. Derby Aviation, as the company was now known, began its first scheduled services from Burnaston in 1953 when a Dragon Rapide flew to Jersey via Birmingham on 18 July of that year.

The Rapide fleet grew to four aircraft, and in 1955 the company took delivery of its first Douglas DC-3 Dakota which went into service on the 3 May when it flew a ship's crew from Manchester to Amsterdam. The following year two 20-seat Miles Marathon aircraft were purchased from West African Airways, and after refurbishment were put into service on the Channel Islands route. With a second Dakota added to the fleet in 1957, the company expanded its operations with a scheduled service to Glasgow and seasonal services from Cheltenham, Gloucester, Luton, Cambridge, Oxford and the Channel Islands.

In 1959 the company was renamed Derby Airways to reflect the changing nature of its activities. The following year the Dakota fleet had increased to six aircraft and added to the revenue figures by delivering Rolls-Royce jet engines made in Derby to airframe manufacturers in Europe - Avons for Caravelles at Toulouse and Darts for Fokker F27 Friendships at Schiphol.

This was a period of rapid expansion for the company, who carried 32,105 passengers during the 1960 season - a hundred per cent increase on the previous year. It soon became evident that the six Dakotas would not be enough and they began looking round for bigger and better equipment which would bring down the seat-mile costs in what was increasingly becoming a competitive business. The choice fell on the Argonaut and, as we now know, proved to be a disastrous one for the airline (see chapter 5).

It was at this time that Derby Airways suffered its first fatal accident. A Dakota, G-AMSW, radio call sign Sierra Whisky, took off from Gatwick at 20:43 on the night of 6 October 1961 bound for Perpignan. The aircraft had been chartered by Whitehall Travel, London, to fly 31 tourists to Perpignan, from where they would continue their journey by coach to Spain.

The flight was seemingly uneventful and the last radio call was made to Bordeaux Control at 00:30 who gave the aircraft clearance to climb to 7,500 feet. But due to a navigational error Sierra Whisky was off course and flying towards Mount Canigou in the Pyrenees.

Andre Maysou, a nightwatchman said:

'During the night of 6 to 7 October, I was on duty at the Le Salve mines when I heard a throbbing noise. Thinking that it was an explosion at the explosives depot of the mine, I went outside and saw it was an aircraft. It was coming from the direction of Ria and heading towards the Canigou Massif. From the sound of the engines it was flying fairly low. I had the impression that this aircraft was lost and that it was going to fly into the Pic Mousquit. Finally I saw it disappear behind this peak and I thought it was safe. I clearly made out steady lights at the aircraft's rear, but did not notice the lighting inside. At the time of its passage the weather was misty and it was raining slightly. I stayed outside for another ten minutes and I did not hear any explosion.'

The crew, unaware of their navigational error, probably never saw the mountain side, and if they did it was too late to take avoiding action. Sierra Whisky knocked off the tops of a number of pine trees before slamming into the rugged rock face. The aircraft completely disintegrated on impact and caught fire, killing all on board. The wrist watches found on the passengers and crew had all stopped at 01:00.

Monsieur Raymond Ribes, a 42 year old lorry driver said,

'On Saturday 7 October, at about 4 o'clock in the morning, I was coming back from Perpignan in my lorry, travelling towards Estoher. On the side of Vinca, I saw to my left on the Canigou slopes a ball of fire. It seemed to me that at times it was brighter and at other times it disappeared from view. At about one and a half kilometres from Estoher, at Espira de Conflent, I stopped and was able to see that this ball of fire was still in the same place. At noon on the same day I heard that a search was being made for an aircraft lost in the vicinity.'

The subsequent investigation by the French Accident Investigation Bureau, stated:

The aircraft was at a flight level below that contained in the operations manual of Derby Airways. The charts on board could have led to the calculation of differing safety altitudes. However, it was not possible to establish what charts were used by the crew. In fact, the airline had not fixed the type of chart to be used for the purpose of applying the formula specified in the operations manual.

In the opinion of the Commission the accident was the result of a navigational error, the origin of which it has not been possible to determine for lack of sufficient evidence.

In October 1964 the airline was renamed British Midland Airways in preparation for the move to the East Midlands Airport at Castle Donington, which was nearing completion. In September 1964, two Handley Page Heralds were ordered at a combined cost of £600,000. Shortly afterwards, BMA acquired the assets of the defunct Mercury Airlines, which provided it with check-in and office facilities at Manchester Airport. Also taken on was Mercury's station manager, Michael Bishop (now Sir Michael Bishop and company chairman).

The first Herald was delivered to Burnaston in February 1965, where British Midland still maintained a presence while engineering work was completed on an Argonaut. The move to East Midlands took place at the end of March 1965.

With further expansion of BMA's services, three BAC One-Eleven 300s were ordered at Farnborough in September 1965, the intention being to retire the Argonauts and all but one of the Dakotas (retaining one for cargo services). However, the contract was cancelled in favour of three Vickers Viscounts purchased from British United Airways in 1966.

In 1967, after the Stockport disaster, the Dakotas and Argonauts disappeared from the scene and the Viscount fleet increased to five. At this time it was becoming evident that increased capital was needed and an approach was made to Minster Assets, who had a holding in Kent-based Invicta Airways. In February 1969 the two airlines merged and in March Michael Bishop, having achieved rapid promotion from Mercury Airlines station manager, was appointed to the board. The Viscount fleet was still growing and by the end of the year had increased to eleven.

In 1969 British Midland lost two Viscounts in accidents exactly one month apart. The first occurred on the morning of 20 February, when Delta Golf operated a scheduled passenger service from Leeds-Bradford Airport to Glasgow. The Viscount departed Leeds-Bradford at 07:45, arriving at Glasgow at 08:45. After a 25 minute stop-over, during which time the aircraft was refuelled, it took off for East Midlands Airport with the same crew on board. Due to the freezing weather prevailing at the time, the propeller and aerofoil anti-icing had been switched on shortly after departing Glasgow, and the protected surfaces were free of ice.

After leaving controlled airspace in the vicinity of Glossop, the aircraft was identified by East Midlands approach control and directed onto a surveillance radar approach for runway 10. Turbulence and a marked wind shear had been reported near the landing threshold of this runway by a pilot who landed at 09:25. This information was passed to the captain, both by East Midlands Air Traffic Control and the pilot of the other aircraft.

During the approach, the airfield weather was passed to the aircraft. This included the Runway Visual Range (RVR) of 900 metres. The windscreen de-icing was switched on during the descent and successfully cleared the port and starboard windscreen panels. The centre panel remained opaque due to a build-up of snow and ice. The captain flew the aircraft manually, concentrating on the instruments until the first officer made visual contact with the runway at 400 feet. The captain, after identifying the runway, considered that the aircraft was not properly positioned to carry out a landing and decided to overshoot and try a second approach.

The captain informed Air Traffic Control, that although he had seen the runway lighting at about half a mile, he had found it very difficult to distinguish between the runway and the snow covered ground, as they tended to blend together. He also announced his intention of diverting to Manchester if the second approach had to be abandoned. The Viscount was again directed by radar for a second approach to runway 10. In the early stage of this approach the co-pilot made visual contact with the ground and reported the runway lights in sight on reaching 350 feet, which was the critical height. Due to the drift angle taken up by the aircraft, caused by the cross-wind, the obscured centre windscreen panel allowed the captain to see only the lights on the left hand side of the runway. To allow him to see the full width of the runway the captain turned the aircraft onto the runway heading. The result of this action was to cause the aircraft to drift to the right. The captain decided that a landing was possible, selected 40 degrees of flap at 300 feet and realigned the aircraft with the runway.

Eyewitnesses on the ground saw that the last stage of the approach was very steep and the aircraft flew onto the runway at a high rate of descent. The nose had just started to rise when the nosewheel struck the runway and collapsed. The main landing gear then slammed onto the runway and the fuselage ruptured at the centre section. The aircraft slewed off the runway to the left and came to rest on snow covered grass. There was no fire and the passengers and crew quickly evacuated the aircraft.

British Midland Viscount Delta Golf

A detailed examination of the wreckage by accident investigators failed to find any evidence of pre-crash failure or malfunction in the aircraft, its engines or equipment, apart from the flight recorder. The recorder was not functioning correctly and there was no record in the log books to indicate when the faulty unit was installed. There was no record of any action taken by British Midland to repair this unit and this situation had existed for some time, possibly in excess of two years.

The accident report stated that the pilot had failed to execute a proper landing flare manoeuvre in adverse weather conditions.

Exactly one month later, on the 20 March, another British Midland Viscount crashed on take-off at Manchester Airport. The aircraft involved - Juliet Alpha - had arrived at Manchester the evening prior to the accident, having been diverted there due to bad weather at Castle Donington, the planned destination. No maintenance was carried out on the aircraft during its time on the ground at Manchester, other than routine servicing and the replacement of a defective navigation light.

At 14:30 on the following day the crew began briefing for a flight to Edinburgh, where the aircraft was to be flown empty to position for a later service to Castle Donington. Just before engine start up at 15:46, Captain Wallace informed the two stewardesses that he intended to use the flight for co-pilot training and that they should not be worried if the handling of the aircraft appeared to be somewhat rough. He gave permission for Miss Wallis, one of the stewardesses, to occupy the jump seat on the flight deck to observe the training. The other stewardess, Miss Timson, elected to remain in the cabin and occupied the rearmost passenger seat on the port side.

Whilst the aircraft was taxiing out to the take-off point for runway 06, Captain Wallace informed Air Traffic Control of his intention to carry out some training, and added that they should not be concerned if they saw anything abnormal during the take-off. ATC acknowledged this information and alerted the fire service for a training standby, which was the standard procedure at Manchester.

At the request of Captain Wallace, ATC gave approval for the aircraft to commence its take-off run from runway 06. The take-off appeared to be normal. After a ground run of approximately 3,000 feet the Viscount became airborne. During the take-off some ground-based observers heard a change of engine note as if one or more engines had been throttled back. Almost immediately after becoming airborne, when the aircraft was at about 15 feet, it was seen to yaw markedly to starboard. The yaw appeared to be corrected, almost "harshly" as one witness (a Viscount pilot) described it. At the same time as the yaw was being corrected, the aircraft appeared to level off momentarily. It then commenced a second steeper climb, during which it also began to roll and turn to starboard. At first the rate of roll was slow but increased rapidly so by the time the aircraft was approximately 200 feet, the wings were vertical. The aircraft continued to roll and the nose began to drop until the aircraft struck the ground 200 yards south of runway 06. Juliet Alpha was destroyed on impact and a severe fire broke out immediately. The two pilots and Miss Wallis were killed instantly. Miss Timson, who was seated at the rear, released her seat belt and made her way to the rear cabin door, which had sprung open on impact, and jumped clear of the wreckage uninjured.

Because of the lack of positive evidence the investigators came to no firm conclusions as to the cause of the accident, other than that control appeared to have been lost by the pilots whilst carrying out a normal routine training exercise.

Captain Wallace was at the time of the Stockport accident British Midland's safety officer and gave evidence at the inquiry.

In 1970 three BAC One-Eleven 119-seater jets entered service on the inclusive tour market. They were joined in April by the first 186-seat Boeing 707 which was put to work on transatlantic charters to New York, Toronto and the Caribbean. However, with the downturn in the inclusive tour market the One-Elevens were withdrawn from service, and in the year ended September 1971 BMA lost £1.67 million. The Viscounts were put back on the Teesside route and seven more were brought from South African Airways. All were in service by June 1972.

The One-Elevens were finally sold in 1973, but by this time the company was firmly established in a new market, leasing Boeing 707s complete with crews, plus engineering and ground staff to other airlines; up to six were in use at any one time. These contracts proved very lucrative and earned the airline £4 million in foreign exchange.

In August 1976 jet services were reintroduced when a leased Douglas DC-9 was assigned to the Teesside service, and a second DC-9 entered service the following year. They sold off the London-Newquay route to Brymon in August 1976, together with a Herald to operate it, and in 1978 began services out of Liverpool. The end of the decade was marked by the management buy-out of the airline by a consortium headed by Michael Bishop, obtaining control of the business from Minster Assets.

In 1979 the airline for the first time carried over one million passengers and applied for licences to operate in direct competition with British Airways, on routes from Heathrow to Glasgow, Edinburgh and Belfast. By the autumn of 1982 five DC-9s were in service and it was at this period that an operational shift away from East Midlands to London began, leasing a 30-seat Shorts 330 to fly connecting East Midlands Heathrow services.

The first Fokker F27 Friendship arrived in 1981, and by the summer of 1984 seven were in service, along with eight DC-9s, three Viscounts and two Shorts 360s. A year later it was decided that the airline needed a new corporate image and in the October a distinctive blue and red livery was introduced.

On the 29 June 1986 British Midland flew its first international jet service, from Heathrow to Amsterdam, after fighting off opposition from the established airlines on the route. The Viscount, which had done more for the airline than any other type, was retired on the 20 February 1988 when a commemorative last flight was operated from East Midlands to Hurn, where many of them had been built. The Viscount's replacement was to be the British Aerospace ATP, for which BM had been the launch customer in 1985. They entered service in May 1988, flying mainly on the East Midlands to Heathrow, Amsterdam and Channel Islands routes. In the meantime, in September 1987, six Boeing 737s were leased and the following year two 737-400 series were delivered. It was one of these that crashed at Kegworth in January 1989.

The aircraft concerned was Mike Echo, which departed London Heathrow at 19:52 as flight BD092 bound for Belfast. Commander of the Boeing was Captain Kevin Hunt, aged 43. He had been with the airline since 1966. On this particular flight he was to work the radio and systems while the First Officer, David McClelland, aged 39, flew the aircraft.

At 20:05 the aircraft was some 20 nautical miles southeast of East Midlands Airport flying towards the Trent VOR beacon, when the passengers noticed smoke seeping into the cabin through the air conditioning and sparks emanating from the port engine. Forward in the cockpit the crew experienced severe vibration and smelled smoke. Disengaging the autopilot, Captain Hunt took control of the aircraft and asked the co-pilot which engine was causing the problem. With some hesitancy he replied, '...it's the right one' . Captain Hunt ordered him to throttle back the engine and within a few seconds the vibration ceased and the smell of smoke lessened. Declaring an emergency, Captain Hunt turned the aircraft onto the approach to East Midlands Airport and lowered the undercarriage and flaps. When the port engine throttle was pushed forward to counteract the drag caused by the landing gear there was no response.

As the crippled Boeing flew low over the village of Kegworth observers on the ground saw a streak of flame coming from the port engine. Beyond the nose the runway approach lighting pierced the night. Captain Hunt desperately tried to maintain height and extend the glide to reach the airport and the waiting emergency services. In the cockpit the number one engine fire warning bell sounded followed by the ground proximity warning klaxon.

Unable to stay airborne the aircraft struck the ground hard, just to the east of the Ml motorway, damaging the main landing gear. Still intact, the airliner smashed through a section of fencing on the eastern edge of the motorway and dropped 30 feet striking the central crash barrier before impacting the embankment on the northbound carriageway. The passenger cabin was extensively damaged with the forward section breaking away and coming to rest at the top of the embankment. Although the fuel tanks ruptured there was no fire and some of the passengers staggered out of the wreckage unaided. Of the 118 passengers on board, 47 died. Miraculously no-one on the ground was killed or injured, which is remarkable considering that the aircraft crossed two busy carriageways of the Ml.

The investigation concluded that the fire was in the port engine, but in their haste in reacting to the emergency, the crew shut down the starboard engine.

British Midland has come a long way in the sixty years since they began operations from a small airfield near Derby. They are now the UK's second largest airline, and the second biggest operator out of Heathrow.

THE PASSENGERS AND CREW ∾

Dorothy Ackroyd
Michael Ayland
Janet Ayland
Herbert Benton
Phyllis Benton
Christine Benton
James Booth
Eliza Booth
Catherine Brooks
Ronald Cowgill
Annie Cowgill
Philip Cruse
Bernard Dowd
Jane Dowd
Sarah Gill
Alice Godwin
Leslie Harland
Marie Harland
Alan Hughes
Kathleen Hughes
Elsie James
Arthur Kemp
Elsie Kemp
Roy Latham
Margaret Latham

Gerald Lloyd (Crew)
Mabel Mellor
Lillian Nolan
Julia Nolan
Eva Owen
Christopher Pollard (Crew)
Arthur Reynolds
Ethel Reynolds
Edward Shaw
Gloria Shaw
Jeremy Shaw
Maxine Shaw
Norman Smart
Jillian Smart
Alexander Smith
Glenise Smith
Arthur Smith
Rachel Smith
David Smith
Harry Stansfield
Joan Stansfield
John Stansfield
Brian Stott
Ann Stott

Alan Taylor
Jean Taylor
Tony Taylor (Crew)
Philip Thorne
Jean Thorne
Peter Thorne
Raymond Tomlinson
Phyllis Tomlinson
Ann Tomlinson
Michael Tomlinson
Thomas Walsh
Jean Walsh
Jeanette Walsh
William Walsh
Gertrude Williams
Paul Williams
Joseph Wilshaw
Marjorie Wilshaw
William Wood
Joan Wood
Reuben Woolfson
Sonia Woolfson
Wendy Woolfson

SURVIVORS ∾

Capt. Harry Marlow
Harold Wood
Mary Green
Susan Howarth (d.1998)

Vivienne Thornber
Bill Wood
Albert Owen
Alan Johnson (d.1995)

David Ralphs
Fiona Child
Julia Partleton (d.1996)
Linda Parry (d.)